Our Daily Spread

Devotions and Encouragement from
One Inmate to Another

Randy Rubingh

Copyright

~ ~ ~

Disclaimer

Dedication

This book is dedicated to my parents. When the unimaginable happened, and we didn't know what to do or how to act, you just held me tight. That's exactly what I needed. Thank you for both the things you said and didn't say. I love you, mom and dad.

And to all those behind jail and prison walls—you are not forgotten and you are not alone.

~ ~ ~

Psalm 66:10-12: For you, God, tested us; you refined us like silver. You brought us into prison and laid burdens on our backs. You let people ride over our heads; we went through fire and water, but you brought us to a place of abundance.

Table of Contents

Table of Contents

Regarding the Title – *Our Daily Spread*

Inmates often get together, combine noodles, chips, canned meat, and anything else available from commissary, mix it together and share it as a meal. This is referred to as a Spread.

Introduction

I used to read the paper and was judgmental about people who made poor and inexcusable decisions that led to them being arrested. I'm not talking about small crimes but big ones with tragic consequences. I thought such people were monsters who deserved to be locked up. But what do you do when one day you are that monster? Unfortunately, I now know what you do. You cling to anyone who can help. Desperately you search for answers and meaning. You cry out to God. After I was arrested I began to cry out to God and these writings are based on those cries of guilt, fear, and shame. I don't have answers, just questions. I hope these writings don't come off sounding like I know how people in jail should act or I have the right to preach in any way. These are simply the result of my working through my two-and-one-half years in jail and trying to make sense out of it.

I have so many people to thank.

- My sons who never gave up on themselves and stood beside me while my actions put them through hell. Nicholas and Christopher I love you so much.

- Marty, the swearing Chaplain. You taught me God is bigger and more loving than I even knew. How can I thank you for that? You taught me humility is the key to the spiritual path. I hope this book honors and reflects that thought.

- Ray, whose visits and help sustained and encouraged me. I miss seeing you every week.

- My cousin Becky who faithfully prayed for me and wrote me long letters every week telling me about her life and that of her ten children. I am forever grateful.

- Joan L, the first line of your first letter read, "Randy we've never met, but I feel like I know you because I pray for you so often." You were one of the first to bring me hope.

- Laurel whose books, letters, and visits were of much and great encouragement.

- Ernie who taught me to maneuver Choices and kept me sane my first year there.

- Jeb who kept me sane the last year I was there.

- And all those who wrote to me, prayed for me, and supported me and my family—I love you all and am forever grateful.

The process of going through my papers and writings has been painful. These are days I would rather leave behind and no longer think about. But to honor those I have hurt greatly, I know I must do anything I can to try and help as many as I am able. If this book does help anyone, I will be grateful, and the process of reliving my pain will have been worth it. To all the men of Choices and those in jail and prison—don't give up. Don't lose hope. Put one foot in front of the other and march in steady time. May God bless you.

Devotionals

God Cares for Prisoners

Isaiah 61:1-2: The Spirit of the Sovereign Lord is on me, because the Lord has anointed me to proclaim good news to the poor. He has sent me to bind up the brokenhearted, to proclaim freedom for the captives and release from darkness for the prisoners, to proclaim the year of the Lord's favor and the day of vengeance of our God, to comfort all who mourn,

God cares about those of us in prison. Sometimes it seems no one cares about us. Politicians talk about the need to enforce tougher sentences and accuse their opponents of being too soft on crime. Guards treat us in a dehumanizing way, constantly reminding us we are prisoners and don't have rights. Sometimes even family and friends tend to neglect us. Our books run out, and no one replenishes them. As time goes on, visits become less frequent, and we get less mail. But as Isaiah reminds us, God doesn't forget us. The Bible continually reminds us God cares for the poor, the disadvantaged, the orphans, and yes, those of us in jail or prison.

I believe God has a special place in His heart for us because while we are here we become more honest and open to Him. While in jail I had nowhere else to turn, so I turned to God. And, even though I'm still in jail, God has freed me from my sins, addictions, and my old way of life. I know he looks out for me, and with his mercy, one day I will walk out of here a free man—free in more ways than one.

God, thank you for the freedoms you have given me even while I am behind bars. Please keep me safe and comfort me until the day I am free from these bars, and with your mercy, on that day, I will truly be free.

Accepting Our Sentence

Job 2:10: He replied, "You are talking like a foolish woman. Shall we accept good from God, and not trouble?" In all this, Job did not sin in what he said.

I spent most of my 2 ½ years of time in county jail in a program called "Choices," modeled after the behavior modification program of Delancy Street in San Francisco, which means there was a lot of yelling and screaming by the counselors to get us to change our behavior. We didn't like this, but the courts looked at the program favorably, and as a sign participants were serious about change, which we all hoped would result in a lighter sentence. To get into the Choices program, inmates had to apply and work through classifications. Many inmates did this, not concerned with improving themselves, but with the sole motivation and hope that being in Choices would help them get that lighter sentence, even potentially being placed into a program instead of prison.

Before sentencing, a large percentage of the inmates were model prisoners attending AA, NA, working jobs, and being positive members of the community. However, many of these same inmates stopped doing these things as soon as sentencing didn't go their way. The same with attending church and Bible studies here in the jail. A lot of people prayed and went to church before sentencing, but when sentencing didn't go their way, they stopped. In one case, an inmate flushed his Bible down the toilet.

These inmates confused God with Santa Claus. They assumed if they were "good," God would change their circumstances. But we need to accept God and His will for our lives even when the circumstances are not what we want and things don't go our way. If we are really submitting ourselves to God and His will, we must stay committed even when things do not go the way we hoped—yes even when sentencing or parole hearings don't go the way we want. Don't get me wrong; this doesn't mean we don't do everything we can to reduce our sentence and reduce our time. It just means when the sentence is longer than hoped, or the parole board denies us, we don't give up our faith and hope in the Lord. *God never promised to get us out of tough times; He promises to be with us through the bad times.*

"Lord please help me to accept my sentence with dignity, grace and purpose –knowing you are in control."

Being Honest with God

Psalm 13:1-2: How long, Lord? Will you forget me forever? How long will you hide your face from me? How long must I wrestle with my thoughts and day after day have sorrow in my heart? How long will my enemy triumph over me?

While in jail, the Psalms took on a whole new meaning to me. Before my arrest I didn't really appreciate or relate to the Psalms. But reading them while in jail, I began to see and understand the honesty of the Psalm writers, especially David. David never hesitates to tell God when he is afraid, frustrated, or upset. He models for us how God wants us to be honest with Him. We don't have to go through pain with a smile on our face just because we are Christians.

In today's passage, David feels God has forgotten him. He talks about having to wrestle with his thoughts. Everyone who has been to prison can relate to having to wrestle with their thoughts. Our minds constantly replay events in our past hoping we do something different, or we future trip, thinking about things that might go wrong, like sentencing for those of us in County Jail. And like David, "day-after-day" we feel sorrow in our hearts. But even in despair, David remembers what God has done for him. He trusts in God. He knows he is saved and is grateful to the Lord. When I am feeling depressed and lost in regret, I find it helps to make a "gratitude list." I write down things the Lord has done for me. Often, this gives me a fresh perspective and improves my mood. But even if it doesn't, like David, I know I can bring my true feelings to God.

Lord, thank you I can be honest with you. Some days in here, I am lonely, depressed, and feel abandoned by you. When those times come, thank you for being patient with me. In those times, please help me and remind me of things I can be grateful for.

Free in Prison

2 Corinthian 3:17: Now the Lord is the Spirit, and where the Spirit of the Lord is. There is freedom.

About a month ago a fellow inmate was released. When he was leaving he talked about being free and how happy he was to be getting out. He was, however, worried he might relapse and start taking drugs again. Sure enough, he is now back here in jail on a new drug charge. He got to have some time on the outside, but he was never really free—he was still addicted to drugs and was destined to come back here. Contrast him with another inmate I know who is three years in on a twenty-year sentence. This man met the Lord here in prison, has completely changed his life, his ways, and his attitude. He is now free from drugs, free from violence, and free from hate. He may not be able to go wherever he wants to, but he is experiencing peace, love, and joy—even while serving a long sentence. He is more free than a lot of people outside these walls. Through Jesus we can experience true freedom—freedom from sin, our old ways, and our pasts. I look forward to the day when I can walk away from this jail. In the meantime, I trust God that it is better to be "free" and in prison, than be on the outside and a prisoner of my old sinful ways.

"Lord, please help me to be truly free. Free from the sin and guilt of my past. Bless me and give me freedom in Christ, even though I spend my days behind bars."

God Has Chosen Us

Isaiah 41:9b-10: I said, "You are my servant;" I have chosen you and have not rejected you. So do not fear, for I am with you; do not be dismayed, for I am your God. I will strengthen you and help you; I will uphold you with my righteous right hand.

In the middle of the night last night some legal documents were delivered to me in my cell. I don't understand them completely, or know what they mean in terms of my charges or eventual sentence. (I'm still in County awaiting trial.) But the documents made me afraid. Afraid that I may be facing even more prison time than I first anticipated. I'm afraid as I see the last of my savings being used for lawyers and knowing when I get out I will have no money. I'm discouraged not knowing when I will get out, where I will have to go to do my sentence, and not knowing how I will survive or where I will live when I eventually get out. At times these thoughts and fears overwhelm me. But today as I was feeling this way, I read these verses from Isaiah. God reminds me that He has chosen me. He has not forgotten us while we are in prison. He is here walking beside us and He gives us strength, even when we feel like we cannot go on.

"Lord, when I am discouraged, please remind me that even here, you are with me. You have a purpose for my life and promise to strengthen me and help me make it through each day. Please send me encouragement and strength. And thank You for choosing me to be Your servant."

God Is with You in Prison

Joshua 1:8-9: Keep this book of the law always on your lips: meditate on it day and night, so that you may be careful to do everything written in it. Then you will be prosperous and successful. Have I not commanded you? Be strong and courageous. Do not be afraid; do not be discouraged, for the Lord your God will be with you wherever you go."

When I first got to jail I was in intake for two weeks and then moved down to a 12-man tank. This was my first time in jail, and as soon as I got to the tank, I was scared. I did not understand the politics and came close to making some serious mistakes. I also wasn't used to being around men who used violence to settle disputes. I felt abandoned by God. But as soon as I could, I got I got a Bible and began to read it and find comfort in it. I knew I would need to read more than a chapter a day to avoid getting caught up in prison life, or at least seriously discouraged by it. I kept my Bible with me and read it two or three times a day. I soon adopted a plan to read ten chapters a day from different parts of the Bible. This meant very day I read something from the Psalms, the Old Testament, the New Testament and the Apostles letters. Through this process I got to know the Bible really well and learn a lot about God. I found other inmates respected this and never antagonized me or gave me any problem for reading the Bible.

I also went to all Christian services (both Bible Studies and Catholic Services). There I found other Christians, many of whom have helped me maneuver through my first four months in prison, which is when I am writing this.

At first I thought God abandoned me when he let my sins lead to my crimes and getting arrested. But I learned God is with me and helping me get through my time in jail. I've heard testimonies where inmates have said "I wasn't arrested. I was rescued... God used the police to get me here to get my attention and save my life—otherwise I would probably be dead by now." That's true for a lot of us inmates. Ask yourself, "How is God trying to get my attention now? Because He is with us.

Yes, God is with us even behind bars.

"Lord be with me today. Remind me of your presence and that you are here with me behind these bars."

Feeling Depressed

Psalm 22:1-2: My God, my God, why have you forsaken me? Why are you so far from saving me, so far from my cries of anguish? My God, I cry out by day, but You do not answer; by night, but I find no rest.

Psalm 27:13-14: I remain confident of this: I will see the goodness of the Lord in the land of the living. Wait for the Lord; be strong and take heart and wait for the Lord.

Most of my time in jail is spent following a routine. As I go through my routine, I try not to think too much about the fact I am locked up and should be enjoying a life outside these walls. But sometimes out of the blue, a feeling will come over me, and it really hits me that I am stuck in jail while life goes on without me. When this happens, it's like a wave of depression and sadness overcoming me. I feel defeated, and to be honest, I feel like crying. Crying over all I have lost, or will lose, crying over my family devastated by me being here, crying over years wasted. Crying over the pain I've caused others. Sometimes when this happens I have trouble finding God's presence. Sometimes He feels so far away. When this happens I often turn to the same Psalm Jesus did when he was on the cross. Like Jesus, I ask God why has He forsaken me? Why do I have no peace? Like the Psalmist, I beg God for an answer. Sometimes something will happen to lift my spirits—a kind word, a reminder I am not forgotten, a chance to help someone. Sometimes these things happen, but not always. Sometimes I am left with no immediate help or response from God. When this happens I have to wait on the Lord. I have to remember that He is good, and one day, I will once again enjoy His presence and mercy. I take heart that He is here, and He is listening.

"Lord, sometimes I am depressed, lonely, and afraid. Please do not be far from me—let me know this is only a season of my life, and it will pass. Give me help and the strength to carry on. Do not let my fears fool me into thinking I am alone. For You are with me and will never forsake me."

Not a Disgrace in God's Eyes

Isaiah 25:8: He will swallow up death forever. The Sovereign Lord will wipe away the tears from all faces; He will remove his people's disgrace from all the earth. The Lord has spoken.

After I was arrested, I began to receive letters and visits from people I knew but hadn't told I had been arrested. They either had learned from mutual friends or, in a couple cases, had seen me on the news. While I appreciated support from anyone willing to offer it, I also often wished not everyone knew about what I had done. I felt humiliated and a disgrace to both myself and my family

But I know God can remove my sin from His eyes and forgive me. And even though I have to endure the consequences of my sin, I should not and do not have to let my crimes or past define me. In God's eyes we are all sinners, but when we accept Jesus, we are all made holy and pure. God does not define us by the worst about us, and we shouldn't let anyone else do that to us either. Yes, some of us have committed horrible crimes, but if we accept Jesus, we are forgiven. While some may continue to label us criminals, we should not define ourselves that way. We cannot change the past, but we can use our past mistakes as a cautionary tale to help others, allowing some good to come from our situations, and changing the narrative of the remainder of our lives. Hopefully doing so has some redeeming power for ourselves and those negatively affected by our actions. Most importantly, we can look forward to the day in Heaven when we no longer feel any disgrace from anyone.

"Lord, please redeem my life. Do not let my past define me; wipe away my disgrace and let me live a life in you that I and my family can be proud of."

Visits

Matthew 25:39-40: "When did we see you sick or in prison and go to visit you?" "The king will reply, 'Truly, I tell you, whatever you did for one of the least of these brothers and sisters of mine, you did for me.'

A visit is always one of the things we most look forward to and hope for while in jail or prison. We long to see our family, our girlfriends, children, or anyone who may take the time to come see us. It breaks up the monotony of prison life, brings us news from the outside, and gives us a reason to stay strong and look forward to getting out. And as we see in today's verses, God honors those who visit us.

But do we always honor our visitors? Often I hear about, and have experienced, visits that go badly. I get it. When someone comes here, we expect sympathy, understanding of our situation, and money on our books. We sometimes fail to appreciate all they are going through both to visit us and be without us on the outside. Visiting someone in jail or prison is a hassle and may require long drives or bus rides to get here. Our visitor may be searched and almost certainly has to wait around to see us, sometimes for hours. When they do make it in, we ask about things we asked them to do and become frustrated if they didn't do them exactly as we asked, or things didn't work out as we expected. We can easily fail to realize that on the outside things rarely go smoothly and if something doesn't go like we asked, we may get upset. Sometimes visits become an argument of who has it worse, us or them. But we need to let go, and not go there. We need to appreciate. We need to remember our loved ones are doing time on the outside along with us. And we need to remember it's us that caused them to go through the problems they are going through. If you are lucky enough to get them, appreciate your visits and visitors. Let go of things you cannot control. Know how hard it is for them. Honor your visitor— God does.

"Lord, if I am lucky enough to have someone to come see me, or talk with me on the phone, help me to honor and appreciate them. While we are together, help me to focus on them, not me."

Don't Grow Weary

Hebrews 12:3: Consider him who endured such opposition from sinners, so that you will not grow weary and lose heart.

Sometimes, in this jail, time moves quickly and days seem to pass, and suddenly, I find it's another month or even another holiday is here. Other times though, time seems to drag on, and I feel like my time in jail will never be over—and I am wasting precious years of my life. To avoid wasting time, I take all the classes I can and attend any meetings to improve myself. Usually these make me feel good, but other times I feel tired and just want to sit on my bunk and feel sorry for myself. But the verse today reminds me that there is hope for those of us who trust the Lord. We are reminded not to lose heart—eventually this time in our lives will be over.

No matter what our circumstances, we should not grow tired of doing the right thing. If we keep putting one foot in front of the other, strive to help the man in front of us, and continue to trust God, time will pass. Eventually, we will get out and be with our loved ones again. I don't think we will ever regret all the things we do behind bars to improve ourselves, or our situation for when we get out—GED classes, AA/NA, college, personal development classes, etc. *The question is not when will we get out, but who will we be when we get out.*

"Lord, sometimes I do feel discouraged. Please lift me up, remind me of all the blessings I have received, even here in jail. Help me never to grow weary of doing good and help me to not lose heart."

Using a Bad Situation

Genesis 50:20: You intended to harm me, but
God intended it for good to accomplish what is
now being done, the saving of many lives.

Joseph's brothers were jealous of him and sold him into slavery.
Years later he is an officer in Pharaoh's court in charge of distributing grain during a famine. The brothers come to buy grain and
eventually Joseph has them move down to Egypt where they will
be safe and have enough to eat during the long famine. Genesis
chapters 37-50 tell the complete story. Today's verse is Joseph
speaking to his brothers because they are afraid that now their father has died Joseph may take revenge on them. But notice how
Joseph, even though he was mistreated and wrongly imprisoned
because of their actions does not hold it against his brothers. Joseph understands although something terrible happened to him,
God was able to use it for good. Unlike Joseph, most of us have
not been imprisoned wrongly. We are here because of choices we
made. But God can still use our imprisonment for good. One day
we may view our time in prison as worth it if, while we are incarcerated, we use our prison experience to change our lives. We can
use this time to get a firm foundation of sobriety, to work on our
education and job skills, or to work through the issues of guilt or
forgiveness that may be preventing us from being our best selves.
We might also do good by being a witness with words or actions
that will help another to experience the Love of God. *Evil may
have brought us to prison, but God can and will use it for good if
we let Him.*

*"Lord, I may be here because of wrong that I have done, but
please use my time in prison for good. Please change me and use
me to let others know about Your love and forgiveness."*

Don't Shrink from Your Story

2 Timothy 1:7-8: For the Spirit God gave us does not make us timid, but gives us power, love and self-discipline. So do not be ashamed of the testimony about our Lord or of me his prisoner. Rather join with me in suffering for the gospel, by the power of God.

In today's verses, the Apostle Paul writes we should be bold in our faith and live by the power of the Holy Spirit. Paul also says not to be ashamed of the gospel or afraid of suffering. I especially like "do not be ashamed of the testimony about our Lord or of me his prisoner." When I read that I think of my own testimony, and how my testimony now includes time spent in jail. Usually we think of time in jail or prison as something to hide and be ashamed of. But it is going to be difficult to hide. I have years of my life that it will be hard to avoid talking about. So rather than avoid it, maybe I can embrace it, especially as it relates to my walk with the Lord. Has the Lord used your time in prison to teach you about Him? Have you started to change your life to be more like Jesus? Has the harsh reality of being locked up changed you so you now appreciate your family and friends on a new and deeper level? Is your story of your relationship with God more interesting now that it includes being in prison? I'll bet it is. God can use your time in prison to change you in a powerful and glorious way if you let Him. As that becomes a part of your story, embrace it. You have an interesting story to live and tell. Others can benefit and learn from your story. Don't shrink from it.

"Lord, I'm ashamed to have done things to get me into jail. But I know that you can and will change me if I let you. Let these changes be real and lasting. When I am released, help me to use my story to help others learn about you and avoid my mistakes. Let me never be ashamed of You or of my story about how You changed me while I was here behind bars."

Getting Sober

Proverbs 20:1: Wine is a mocker and beer a brawler; whoever is led astray by them is not wise.

Almost everyone I have met here in jail is here because of drugs or alcohol. At an AA meeting in jail last night, the speaker said ninety-five percent of the people in jail were here for a drug offense, a crime to get money to buy drugs, or were at least loaded when they were arrested. That sounds about right based on talking with people here. So, the first order of business in getting out and not coming back to jail has to be getting clean and sober. We convicts cannot expect to reconcile with our families, be able to hold down a job, or stay out of prison unless we remain off of drugs and alcohol. Recovery needs to start for us in jail now. Do not wait until you are out to go to a recovery program or AA or NA meetings. If there is a program within the jail you are at, start it now. If there are 12-step meetings, attend all you can. Drugs and pruno are available in prison, but do everything you can to avoid them, and those that use them. Recovery needs to start now and continue when you get out. When you get out, it becomes harder, not easier, to stay clean. So establish sober living habits now, so when you get out you won't relapse.

"Lord, please help me in my recovery. I know I cannot serve both you and drugs. Be the Lord of my life to help me to live a clean and healthy life with friends and family. Help me to make the tough decisions about who I associate with, both now and upon my release."

A Kind Word

Proverbs 12:25: Anxiety weighs down the heart, but a kind word cheers it up.

Anyone who has ever been inside knows how important it is to watch your tongue. The wrong word or showing a lack of respect can set someone off and is dangerous. On the flip side, a kind word goes a long way on the inside. We are constantly bombarded with negativity, and life as an inmate is dehumanizing. We are treated as a number and constantly reminded about our lack of status and lack of freedom. That's why it goes so far when someone uses a kind word. Recently when I said "Good morning; How are you?" to an inmate, he replied "Blessed to be alive." That got me thinking about how I need to be grateful, and I mentally made a list of things I could be grateful for. This gave me a quick mental reset and brightened my attitude. The next day I told the inmate how he had helped improve my mood by his simple response. Later, he told me that telling him how he had encouraged me in turn lifted his spirits. A positive cycle of encouragement had been started by his simple reply.

Everyone craves a kind word, especially those on the inside who hear them so rarely. Think about the positive impact you can have with a few kind words.

"Lord, help me to spread a kind word today. Let me be known as an encourager. I pray you send me someone who needs a kind word today, and I can be your instrument."

Not Fearing Authority

Proverbs 1:32-33: For the waywardness of the simple will kill them, and the complacency of fools will destroy them; but whoever listens to me will live in safety and be at ease, without fear of harm."

Yesterday we had a raid. We were all hustled down to the yard, and as we left, we saw a dozen deputies walking in with gloves on and dogs. We knew a search was about to happen. But unlike some other times when I have been in similar situations, I was at peace. I knew I had no contraband or anything else I wasn't supposed to have. At first, just the idea of the raid made me tense and resentful. But I decided to change my attitude, and instead of focusing on the raid, to just enjoy the extra time out in the fresh air of the yard. I knew I had nothing they would find that would lead to a write-up or punishment. I was "at ease without fear of harm."

I do not like the raids. We are presumed guilty, and many times it seems like guards are taking out their personal frustrations on us. They have no respect for our personal property. Sure enough when I returned to my cell it had been completely ransacked—I would have to reorganize my stuff, remake my bed, etc. While I do not like feeling this way, I do like not having to be afraid of authority. So many times on the outside if I was stopped, I was thinking of excuses or lies because I knew I had done something wrong. I do not like these raids but I am at ease "without fear of harm," from authorities. And it is a much better way to live.

"Lord, help me to live my life in such a way I do not have to fear authority."

Don't Waste Your Incarceration

Proverbs 6:6-11 or 9-11: Go to the ant, you sluggard; consider its ways and be wise! It has no commander, no overseer or ruler, yet it stores its provisions in summer and gathers its food at harvest. How long will you lie there, you sluggard? When will you get up from your sleep? A little sleep, a little slumber, a little folding of the hands to rest—and poverty will come on you like a thief and scarcity like an armed man.

When I was locked up at County, we took it in every day for count at 4:30 p.m., and resumed rec at 7:00. Most people napped during this time. Actually, most people napped not only then, but whenever we took it in—two or three times a day. I don't think that biblically or spiritually there is anything wrong with taking advantage of these times to catch up on sleep. But I would challenge if sleeping at every opportunity during the day is good use of an inmate's time. Personally, I avoided napping because I wanted to be able to fall asleep quickly when I turned in for the night. I found if I wasn't tired enough, my thoughts would wander toward guilt, regret, anxiety, and worry. So, not napping helped me to go to sleep faster and be in a better state of mind.

Secondly, I try to make better use of my time. In fact, much of this book, including what I am writing now, was written as

I waited for count while my cellie and most inmates slept. Even if I wasn't spending my time on spiritual things like Bible reading or prayer, I tried to better myself by doing homework from classes or reading good books. I encourage you to try and make good use of your time. Of course, sometimes you will want or need to sleep or spend time at rec watching movies or playing cards or chess. But if that's all you ever do, and you come out the same person you entered as, your incarceration will have been wasted. Try to spend some time every day improving yourself.

Make the most of your time; prepare yourself for your future.

"God help me to make the best use of my time possible. I cannot always be productive, but help me to prepare for my future by using my down time to learn about you or improve myself."

Worrying

Mathew 6:34: Therefore do not worry about to-morrow, for tomorrow will worry about itself. Each day has enough trouble of its own

As I write this, I have now been in County Jail for eight months, and I have three more months until my pre-trial conference. Around me, friends take deals and go to sentencing. Some are blessed and receive programs or light sentences. Others go to reception at San Quentin to start ten-to-thirty-year sentences. What really frightens me is when someone signs a deal with a wide range. For example, one friend just signed a probation bottom with an eight top. An eight top may (or may not) sound like much to you, but it's the range that scares me, giving the judge that much power to either send you to a program and start the road to freedom, or leaving for San Quentin to start eight years. We're praying for mercy for this brother. But what is most inspiring is, although he is stressed and afraid, he knows God has perfect timing. He knows God has a plan for him, although he earnestly hopes it's not to be sent away; he is trusting God. Trusting God to be with him no matter what and that he will be freed in God's perfect timing.

"Lord, please give me the strength and faith of my friend John. I miss not being home with my family. But help me to trust Your timing on when I am released.

Living in the Present

Ecclesiastes 7:10: Do not say, "Why were the old days better than these?" For it is not wise to ask such questions.

Our minds spend a lot of time dwelling on the past. Often it's reliving "glory days," or in the case of a lot of us in jail or prison, simply replaying in our heads over and over the incidents that led to our arrests. As I look back over that fateful night I was arrested, there were so many things that could have happened differently that would have resulted in me not being in that place at that time. But I made certain wrong choices, and I was there. As much as I may regret it, and as remorseful as I am, I cannot change the past. I can learn from it, but it does not change. It does no good to let our minds continually replay those events. In fact, it's bad for our health to continually replay those stressful times.

I practice mindfulness and meditation to try as much as possible to live in the present. If I find myself daydreaming about the past, I simply remind myself that it is done, and I need to go forward from where I am today. I know if I spend too much time in the past, I may miss what's going on around me now. As the Serenity Prayer says, "God grant me the serenity to accept the things I cannot change, the courage to change the things I can, and the wisdom to know the difference."

"Lord, help me not to dwell on the past. Show me what You want me to do today. Show me how to love the person directly in front of me now."

From Shame to Honor

Isaiah 61:7: Instead of your shame you will receive a double portion, and instead of disgrace
you will rejoice in your inheritance. And so you
will inherit a double portion in your land, and
everlasting joy will be yours.

We deserve shame. We did wrong, maybe a lot of
wrong, and we are in jail or prison. Most of us deserve the sentences we receive. But God does not
want to shame us. He wants us to be repentant for sure, but
once forgiven, He does not want us to wallow in our sin. I have
sons. When one of them does something wrong I want them to
say they're sorry and try their best not to do it again. But the
last thing I want is for them to beat themselves up over whatever they did. I want to restore them, to make them feel good
about themselves again. That's how to get them back on the
right track. God doesn't want us to feel shame either. He wants
to restore us as His children. He wants to get us back on track.
In fact, instead of shame, He promises us an inheritance.

In this verse He's telling us not to become depressed over our
sin. Once we've repented He wants us to accept and enjoy His
incredible mercy. I have sinned greatly it's true, but it's also
true I have received enough grace and mercy through the cross
to completely restore me allowing me to seek His will with
confidence, as an heir to the Kingdom.

*"Lord, thank You that although I have sinned much, I have been
forgiven much. And while I may be in jail as the consequence of*

my sins, I am free in You. Please help me to live out this truth despite the guilt I feel."

Truth Sets You Free

Psalm 32:3-5: When I kept silent, my bones wasted away through my groaning all day long. For day and night your hand was heavy on me; my strength was sapped as in the heat of summer. Then I acknowledged my sin to you and did not cover up my iniquity. I said, "I will confess my transgressions to the Lord," and You forgave the guilt of my sin.

The old saying "The truth will set you free" does not mean confessing your crimes will get you out of jail. Although it's true confessing sometime leads to a better deal than losing in trial. Sometimes, that is, but not always, I think we all know when it comes to our cases, it's better to let our lawyers do the talking. But the truth can set you free from anxiety, stress, and the fear of being found out. When I have done something and try to hide it or lie about it, it eats me up inside. I can't help but continue to worry about it, and be afraid of potential consequences. And very often, once the truth comes out, the consequences are not as bad as we feared.

It's often a relief to not have to hide anything. Sometimes we can get in more trouble trying to hide the truth then we would have been in for simply confessing the truth. There's an old saying, "It's not the crime; it's the cover-up." This is often true. Even if it's not true in terms of jail or prison time, it is true in terms of how we feel about and view ourselves. Once I was arrested and my crimes were made public, in one sense it was a relief. There was no longer a reason to try and hide anything about myself. People knew the worst about me. I knew those that chose to stand by me and support me were true friends.

"Lord, help me to be a man of truth. Help me to live in such a way I don't have a need to lie or cover-up things about myself. Set me free from hiding my past."

An Honest Friend

Proverbs 27:6: Wounds from a friend can be trusted, but an enemy multiplies kisses.

We all like friends who compliment us and tell us good things about ourselves. And it's true being an encourager is an important aspect of being a good friend. But what truly benefits us is friends who are willing to tell the truth to us and about us, even when it's something we don't want to hear. Think about it. If someone had taken the chance to tell us we needed to change our behavior, we might have avoided jail.

But most of the time our friends simply agree with us. In turn, we tell our friends what they want to hear. This is not being a true friend. True friends tell each other the truth, even when it's uncomfortable. True friends listen to each other even when it hurts. Next time a friend tells you something you don't want to hear, before you get upset take a minute to think about if they may be right. If they are, thank them for it, and listen carefully to their advice. And if you want to be a true friend to someone, take the chance to tell them something that will benefit them, even if their initial reaction may be to be upset with you.

"Lord, please send me Brothers in Christ to be true friends. Help us brothers to be honest with each other and in the spirit of love help each other to be better Christians and people."

What Do We Really Need?

Acts 3:6-7: Then Peter said, "Silver or gold I do not have, but what I do have I give you. In the name of Jesus Christ of Nazareth, walk." Taking him by the right hand, he helped him up, and instantly the man's feet and ankles became strong.

B eing in prison often feels like we have been reduced to beggars. I just finished writing a letter and debated for a long time if I should end the letter with asking for money for my books. The thing is, I am about out of money and people on the outside, even those willing to help, need to be asked, and I am not comfortable asking. I've always viewed myself as a man who could provide for himself and his family. But now I have no way to provide for myself, and unless others help me, I will go without commissary. I hate this feeling that I have become a beggar. I sometimes pray God will put it on someone's heart to provide for me without me having to ask.

But is commissary what I truly need? While it is certainly nice to have, what I really need from God is not commissary but to help me walk as a man of spiritual principles, walk as a Christian in the yard, walk without getting caught up with people around me. What I really need is simply to walk with Jesus. Commissary and other things are nice to have, but it's not what I really need.

"Lord, please help me to walk with You. Please help me realize that is really all I need today."

Shrinking from Responsibility

1 Samuel 10:22b: And the Lord said, "Yes, he has hidden himself among the supplies."

Saul had been chosen by God and anointed by the prophet Samuel to be the first King of Israel. But when the time comes for him to be revealed as king, he gets scared, shrinks from the responsibility, and "hides among the supplies." What have you been called to do? Have you been called to be a good father, son, or employee? Have you been called to serve the Lord as a peacekeeper in your community? We may have failed in some of these (that's why I'm at least in jail.) But I believe God is calling us now to represent Him wherever we are—even if it's in jail or prison. Let's not shrink from His call. Let's live with integrity while we are here. Let's not hide as Jesus calls us to better ourselves. Let's stand up now so that when we get out we are better men. God calls us all to be sober, men of integrity, and if we have children, to be faithful and loving fathers. Heed the call. Do not be scared or try to hide.

"Lord, I know you are calling me to be a man of integrity. Help me not to be afraid or shrink from my responsibilities."

Growing Spiritually While in Prison

2 Corinthians 4:16 Therefore we do not lose heart. Though outwardly we are wasting away, yet inwardly we are being renewed day by day.

I am trying hard not to waste my time in prison. I know people on the outside fear I am just sitting here wasting away. Sometimes I feel like that myself. But each day I am here I try to learn a little more about God and I try to draw closer to Him. I try to spend some time each day in Bible reading, prayer, and in meditation. I know each day I do these things it's profitable to me. I know that I am growing stronger spiritually. So to those on the outside it may appear that years of my life were wasted, but I try not to look at it that way. I try to look at it as time I was able to spend being renewed each day and growing.

I certainly don't do it perfectly, and I suffer many set-backs, mostly being depressed from missing my family. But each day I get up and look to the Lord to renew me and make it a day of growth.

"Lord, even if my body is suffering while I am in here due to loneliness and sometimes depression, let me continue to develop my spiritual muscles. Help me to grow closer to You and renew a right spirit in me each day."

Ordinary Men, Extraordinary God

Acts 4:13: When they saw the courage of Peter and John and realized that they were un-schooled, ordinary men, they were astonished and they took note that these men had been with Jesus.

On paper, Peter and John appear quite ordinary. They were fishermen by trade and had little education. People didn't expect much from these common men. That's why when people saw and heard them, they were amazed at the things they said and did. But two things set Peter and John apart from everyone else. They had courage, and they had met Jesus. With these qualities, they became two of the most influential men who have ever lived.

You may lack an education, but if you have courage and have met Jesus, you too are capable of doing extraordinary things. God often chooses those who have hard and difficult lives and come from poor circumstances to do important work for His kingdom. All you really need is to know Jesus and have the courage to take steps of faith. Those steps of faith may start small—being honest with other people, avoiding the negativity and temptations of jail/prison, and maybe even telling your cel-lie about how Jesus has affected your life. But if you continue to walk with Jesus and let him use you, you will be surprised at how far He might take you. Particularly, those of us who are or have been in prison have so much opportunity to be used by God to help others in similar circumstances. Be bold. Let Jesus use you today.

"Lord, thank you that you choose people in humble circumstances, like prison, to do mighty things for You. Help me never to use my lack of education or being poor as an excuse to not step out in faith. Help me to be bold and please use me to do Your work."

Refined by Prison

Psalm 66:10-12: For you, God, tested us; you refined us like silver. You brought us into prison and laid burdens on our backs. You let people ride over our heads; we went through fire and water, but you brought us to a place of abundance.

In this Psalm, the writer talks about how when God tests us and we go through trials, we have the opportunity to come out refined like silver. He says although we've been in prison and through fire and water, when we get through it, we can come to a place of abundance. This reminds me of how character is often built in our lives. We always wish for comfort and things to be easy for us, but when we look back on our lives, our times of growth and character building came not when things were going well, but in difficult times. It's only when we face challenges that we grow stronger. We have to strain and break down muscles for them to rebuild stronger.

I've never felt more broken down then now when I'm in jail. It often feels like I'm literally going through fire and water, but I know God can use this time to build my character if I will let Him. The day-to-day challenges we face as prisoners we can either use to become bitter or to allow ourselves to be refined. If we can learn to manage our attitudes and live for Him in these circumstances, we will have the abundance of peace in Him that He promises.

"God, I am going through a trial in jail. I am often discouraged, bored, and afraid. Please use this time to build my character, refine me like silver, and give me an abundance of peace, joy, and hope."

Holding Our Heads High

> Leviticus 26:13: I am the Lord your God, who brought you out of Egypt so that you would no longer be slaves to the Egyptians; I broke the bars of your yoke and enabled you to walk with heads held high.

I am deeply remorseful and ashamed of the events that led me to jail. I had never been arrested or in any kind of trouble before. I also find it incredibly embarrassing as I find out more people from my past learn about what happened, and that I am now in jail. It seems every week I hear about a new group of friends or acquaintances who didn't know but found out. I know I am the subject of a lot of gossip and talk. To be fair, many of these friends are genuinely concerned and when they hear about me, they offer their support and encouragement. I also know when I get out I will need to explain what happened in job interviews, with friends who haven't yet heard, and new friends and acquaintances who will ask about my past while making casual conversation, not expecting my past includes committing an inexcusable act and spending time in jail.

God says that he can break our yoke (relieve our burdens) and allow us to hold our heads high. He says once we turn to Him, we do not need to be ashamed of our past. He will restore us and allow us to hold our heads high. While I may never be the same and I will always be remorseful, I look forward to the day I can say I learned from this experience and became a better man. I hope one day to hold my head high once again.

"Lord, please relieve me of my burden of guilt and shame. Help me to hold my head high in the knowledge that no matter what I've done, You can forgive and use me for good."

Mere Talk

Proverbs 14:23: All hard work brings a profit,
but mere talk leads only to poverty.

When in prison, everyone says when they get out they will change their ways and lead a straight life. In the jail program I am in while writing this, everyone also says the same thing about drugs and alcohol. They say they are committed to being clean and sober and won't use drugs or alcohol once they get out. But the sad fact is about eighty per cent of the people in jail will return to being users—they will relapse and start using again. In the six months I have been here, I already know of at least four people who have been released and returned to jail.

What is the difference between those who are able to stay out and those that return? I think those that stay out are those that are willing to do the work of recovery. Those that begin attending 12-step meetings while in jail are doing work. Those that work on their education or develop job skills while incarcerated are doing work. If you truly want to change, you need to start doing it now, not wait until you're released. People who tell me they will change later, but aren't willing to start today, are exhibiting "mere talk that leads to poverty"

"Lord, help me to be a doer, not someone who merely talks about changing his or her life. Help me to start making changes today that will keep me sober and help me be the best version of myself when I get out."

The Most Important Judge

Isaiah 3:13: The Lord has taken his place in court, he rises to judge the people.

I am not sure I have even been more scared than I was when I went for sentencing before the judge. With one swing of the gavel, the judge changes your life. For those with a modifiable sentence, it's the difference between a program and prison. With one word, the judge determines your fate and how years of your life will be spent. The day of sentencing is truly terrifying. Some people come back from the sentencing elated, having been given a second chance, while others come back disappointed knowing they are now headed for years in prison.

But God is the judge for eternity. If we could grasp this concept and truly understand it, it would change our lives. Eternity is infinitely longer than even multiple life sentences. Nothing on earth can be compared to eternity. And here is the amazing part—for those of us who know Jesus as our Lord and Savior, we have already reached a deal—a plea bargain with God. Our Judge, God, will simply confirm our deal of being forgiven and let us enter into Heaven for eternity. We have nothing to fear as we stand before the most awesome and powerful judge.

Lord, thank You that we already know how You will judge us. Thank you that You will grant us mercy on judgment day and forgive all our sins. Thank You that although I may fear earthly judges, I do not have to fear You, the Judge that truly matters.

One in Christ

Galatians 3:26-28: So in Christ Jesus you are all
children of God through faith, for all of you
who were baptized into Christ have clothed
yourselves with Christ. There is neither Jew nor
Gentile, neither slave nor free, nor is there male
and female, for you are all one in Christ Jesus.

The other day I received a letter from a friend who is
currently in reception at San Quentin. He told me on
the yard the other day there was a prayer circle that in-
cluded all races. Usually, of course, this doesn't happen because of prison politics. I am not sure what the occasion was,
but the thought of it was very comforting as I am in County
and likely will be going to reception in San Quentin soon. It's
great to know that there are times when brothers in Christ can
come together even in prison. Here in the county jail program
I am in, there are no politics allowed. As a result, I have gotten
to meet and worship with people of all races and backgrounds.
It's amazing to see how God is relevant to everyone regardless
of background and ethnicity, and it has been encouraging to get
to know men who have been changed by God—men I never
would have gotten to know in the upper-middle class church I
was a member of before my arrest where almost everyone was
white. Here in jail—Hispanic, black, white, rich, poor—we
come together as equals—all sinners in need of God's grace.
Being in orange, none of us feel more superior than another.
There are no pretenses or posturing here such as is sometimes

found in churches on the outside. It's a blessing to find an authentic and diverse group of brothers here.

"Lord, thank you for helping me experience real church—church without prejudices or pretense while I am here behind bars. Please help others incarcerated to find similar communities in the jails or prisons they are in."

Stop Complaining

Philippians 2:14-15: Do everything without grumbling or arguing, so that you may become blameless and pure, "children of God without fault in a warped and crooked generation." Then you will shine among them like stars in the sky.

Today while I was out in the pod, I caught myself grumbling—complaining. Complaining about the boredom, complaining about the food, complaining with a friend about our lives here on the inside—how awful it is. It occurred to me that when I am complaining, two things happen—First, it makes my attitude even worse. I begin to see everything in a negative light and find even more things to complain about. Second, I become like so many people here in jail—negative and difficult to be around. I lose "my shine." But when I concentrate on all the things the Lord has blessed me with, I become a positive person. I become someone people want to be around. I become someone who encourages others. And with my "light shining like a star in the sky," I open myself up to being used by God. The prison chaplain here has challenged me to write a daily gratitude list. I've noticed that each day I do it, I focus on my many blessings and no longer spend time complaining—well, not nearly as much time anyways.

"Lord, thank You for all the blessings You've given me, even while I am here in jail. Please help me to focus my attention on these things and give me a grateful heart. Help my attitude to be positive and "shine like the stars."

Stop the Bleeding

Mark 5:28-29: because she thought, "If I just touch his clothes, I will be healed." Immediately her bleeding stopped and she felt in her body that she was freed from her suffering.

Before I was arrested and when I was in the business world, I would often use the expression "first stop the bleeding." By this I meant we needed to first stop whatever problem we were having from getting worse, and once that was done we could go clean up whatever damage was done. Like the suffering woman, when we encounter Jesus, the bleeding stops. We still have damage to clean up. We still have prison sentences to serve. We still have amends to make. But at least, if we have Jesus, the bleeding has stopped.

This also doesn't mean everything is suddenly going to go perfectly for us, but it does mean that we can stop living in despair and without hope. It means we now are playing for the winning side. It means we are assured of our salvation, and no matter what else happens to us, we know God will be with us. Since my encounter with Jesus, I know my sins are forgiven, but I still make mistakes. I still have to deal with the consequences of my actions, and I still have to be in this cell, but I am confident now that the bleeding has stopped, my life has purpose and I am moving forward in the right direction.

"Lord, thank You for stopping the bleeding in my life. Thank You for forgiving my sins and giving me a hope I can be of use to You in the future."

God Finds Us in the Storm

Nahum 1:3b: His way is in the whirlwind and
the storm, and clouds are the dust of his feet.

I'm sitting in my cell while we are on lock down, playing
Sudoku, and wondering is this really my life? Will I really
be doing this for years to come? Can I really not leave?
I've been here for over eight months. You would think I would
be over the shock by now, but I wonder if I ever will. Sometimes I can't believe I am "trapped" here while on the outside,
life goes on. Friends and family go about their lives, while my
life has shrunk to a 10 x 6 cell with just reading and doing Sudoku puzzles.

But I do know God is with me. I do know he will not forsake
me. I do know He is real in a way I never knew before. I know
I need to trust and rely on Him in ways I didn't when I was on
the outside. I know Him in a way I didn't before. The way to
God, truly living for God, meant I had to go to this jail experience. I wish I could have found God when my life was peaceful, and I was enjoying my family and a good career, but I did-
n't. His way to get me on a better course was through the storm.
So here I am in the whirlwind, and He is here with me.

*"God, I'm sorry my bad decisions created this storm in my life,
but I thank You that instead of abandoning me You have
reached out to me and rescued me. Thank You that Your ways
are often in the whirlwinds of our lives."*

Lockdown

Ephesians 5:16: making the most of every opportunity, because the days are evil.

I was on rec and the cry came out — "Lock Down. Everyone return to your cells!" Of course, we have no idea why, what's going on, or how long it will last. Usually at this facility, it's short duration, but it sometimes it lasts the rest of the day. Lockdown always serves as a stark reminder we have such little control over our lives in here. We go where and when we are told. We are kept in the dark and treated like we don't even deserve to know what is going to happen to us from one minute to the next. At times like this, I try to concentrate on what I do know and can do. I know I am in the Lord's hands, and I can use time to pray or read the Bible. Everyone who has been inside knows one of our main enemies is boredom and lockdown means boredom and maybe searches. But, while I may be bored, I also do something I did far too little of on the outside: I relax, meditate, and wait on the Lord. I wait to see what I might learn from some reflective, quiet time, even if it's forced and unplanned.

Lord, when I'm locked down, help me not to dwell on what little freedom I have. Instead, let me use this time to focus on You. Help me to live a reflective life and learn to be patient, still, and aware of your presence.

Memorizing Scripture

Proverbs 3:1-4: My son, do not forget my teaching, but keep my commands in your heart, for they will prolong your life many years and bring you peace and prosperity. Let love and faithfulness never leave you; bind them around your neck, write them on the tablet of your heart. Then you will win favor and a good name in the sight of God and man.

When I was a child, I attended church and we would often memorize Bible verses. When I got older, I stopped memorizing verses and forgot much of what I had memorized as a child. In jail though, I have started memorizing again. I don't always have my Bible with me when I am stressed or afraid, but I can always recall a verse I have memorized.

The other day, some men were getting ready to go to court and I was able to share with them some encouraging verses I had memorized (Jeremiah 29:11-14). Memorizing verses is also a good way to meditate on scripture and really get to understand its meaning. The process of memorizing focuses one's mind.

Set a goal for yourself to memorize one or two verses a week that speak to you. Each week, review the verses you have memorized and try to add one or two more. It may help you to make flashcards you can use to help you learn the verses.

Consider starting by memorizing Proverbs 3:1 to remind yourself the importance of this practice. I think you'll be amazed at how helpful this will be in helping you to stay focused on the Lord.

God, I know Your words are important. Please help me to memorize Your word and bring it to my mind when I need it.

Among Wolves

Matthew 10:16: "I am sending you out like sheep among wolves. Therefore, be as shrewd as snakes and as innocent as doves.

In the program I am in, in County Jail, there are no politics. But there were politics in the other pods of the jail I was in before I was moved to this floor. Also, I've spent a lot of time asking questions to inmates who have been to San Quentin about the politics there, because I am afraid of making a mistake if and when I am sent there. To me, "being as shrewd as snakes but as innocent as doves" speaks of how to live in a prison environment where one has to be concerned about the politics. Every place is different, so I cannot speak as to how to maneuver at different places. But, being shrewd means being aware. We need to be aware. We need to learn how to live and survive in a prison environment. On the other hand, we need to be "innocent as doves" not getting caught up in the drugs, violence, or general negativity of prison life. If I am placed in a prison with politics, I will seek to be aware, understand what I need to do, but at the same time, know that ultimately I am in Christ's care. God is the ultimate key holder and He is the one we need to pay the most respect to.

Lord, help me to be smart about who I associate with. I know there are barriers that only You can break down. Give me guidance and help me to maneuver through this environment safely, and in a way that honors You.

Counting the Days

Psalm 39:4: "Show me, Lord, my life's end and the number of my days; let me know how fleeting my life is.

Inmates coming towards an end of a sentence count down the days different ways—some count each day, others Fridays only, some commissary days. There are many ways to mark time. *We may count our days, but it's more important to make our days count.* Each day is an opportunity to serve the Lord and make it count for Jesus. The days count—the years don't. When we are done with our sentences the most important question is what did we do with our time, not how much time did we do.

In AA/NA they say the key to staying clean is to live clean one day at a time. That's also how we should do our sentence. Each day we should strive to live that day the right way. If we do this, although some days may seem long, the years will pass quickly. In addition, I know many stories of inmates who are moving to lower-level yards, some who have had their time reduced, and others being granted early parole. These things didn't happen because they did one thing. They happened because they chose to do the right thing each and every day.

"Lord, help me make today count. My release date may be years away, but today I commit to live for You like it's my last day."

Stories in Our Head

Proverbs 3:5: Trust in the Lord with all your
heart and lean not on your own understanding;

Today we had to participate in an earthquake drill. This
meant we would be shackled together, marched down-
stairs by guards past intake and watched by an obser-
vation group in charge of the drill, and then led back upstairs.
I was not looking forward to this. I always find being shackled
humiliating. I resent the superiority exhibited by the guards,
intake stirs up bad memories, and having this observer group
made me feel like a zoo animal. But as I went through this experience I realized much of the negativity I was feeling was in
my head and I had the power to change the experience.

I realized it's my imagination that associates humiliation with
shackles—in of themselves, they have no definition. I can
choose to not associate humiliation with the shackles and instead simply think of the chains as an item that keeps me in an
orderly line, and not associate any negative feelings with them.

In my mind, before I even interact with them, I view the guards
as having an attitude of superiority over me. This makes we
instantly want to wish I could let them know I am better educated and used to make a lot more money than they do. But this
is just my own insecurity. Maybe some of them do have feelings of superiority, but I do not know this before I interact with
them—I am projecting my insecurity into their minds, an action within my control.

Similarly, the intake room does bring back memories. But I can choose not to relive the fear of when I was in this room being processed after my arrest. Instead as I walk through I can simply observe it. I see a movie of me in the room from when I was first arrested, but I can choose to view it objectively, like reading a history book—it contains facts, images, but not emotion. I can exist in this room without reliving the worst night of my life.

I observe the observers. If I think they are looking at us as inmates and judging us, I am interjecting a story into their heads. I don't know this is true. It's probably more likely they are simply concerned about doing their job and not thinking about us as inmates. Everyone has their own thoughts and fears; I don't need to create a story in my head that they are thinking about me and judging me.

Yes, today I went on an earthquake drill and it has the potential to fill my head with negativity, as I could dwell on humiliation and insecurity, or I could simply take a walk up and choose not to inject negative stories in my head.

"Lord my mind often plays tricks on me, injecting into my head what other people are thinking about me. But too often the story I make up in my head is a negative one. Help me to be able to clear my mind and worry about only what is real, not imagined.

59

Don't Run from Your Story

> John 5:7-9: "Sir," the invalid replied, "I have no
> one to help me into the pool when the water is
> stirred. While I am trying to get in, someone
> else goes down ahead of me." Then Jesus said
> to him, "Get up! Pick up your mat and walk."
> At once the man was cured; he picked up his
> mat and walked. The day on which this took
> place was a Sabbath.

Jesus heals a man at the pool and tells him to pick up his mat and walk. During Jesus' time, carrying a mat on the Sabbath was considered work, and work was forbidden on the Sabbath. But Jesus instructs the man specifically to carry his mat. This is the mat the man has lain on for thirty-eight years hoping for a miracle. The mat is a reminder to the man of all the time he was looking for a miracle, but learned the miracle he needed was Jesus.

Our time in prison may be our mat. It's a part of our story. Like the man in these verses, Jesus may use our mat to remind us of where we've come from, and possibly to inspire others. When I get out of jail, I could try to run from my past—move away, make all new friends who don't know I've ever been to jail, pretend it never happened. But I think Jesus wants to use it as part of my testimony on how this time changed me, and hopefully that can in some way help or inspire others. Jesus can redeem our past if we carry our mat and not try to hide it.

"Lord, although being in jail has been a painful time, let me always remember the lessons You taught me here. If in any way these lessons can be valuable to others, please use me and my story of having gone to jail to help anyone who could benefit."

Love Is an Action

James 2:16: If one of you says to them, "Go in peace; keep warm and well fed," but does nothing about their physical needs, what good is it?

For much of my life, I had empathy and a desire to help and work with people that society would consider less fortunate than myself. I read a lot about church groups that work with the homeless, drug addicts, or those in prison. I admired people who helped these groups, but was afraid to get involved myself. I wasn't sure I could relate to them and to be honest, was uncomfortable around people different than myself. Now that I am in jail, I realize and see how similar we all are. Almost everyone has similar dreams—being able to support and care for their families and being able to make a decent living. Before I came here, I often hesitated to get involved. I hope, though, when I eventually leave here, life for me will be getting involved. I want to become a doer and not just a thinker. Of course, though, if I really want to help others, I need to start now. There are plenty of opportunities I have to demonstrate love right here, right now. I can listen to someone who needs a sympathetic ear. I can offer encouragement and support others when they are going through it, as happens so often here. There are many ways to get involved and help others, even here in jail.

Lord, help me to take action to show love to someone today. Help me not to hesitate or wait when I see someone who could use my help.

Seeing My Son

Proverbs 23:24: The father of a righteous child has great joy; a man who fathers a wise son rejoices in him.

Yesterday I had a visit from my son. It was a joy to see him. I have been here one year and this was the fourth time he has come. Because he is fourteen, he is going through a growth spurt, and his physical appearance changes each time I see him. When he visits, it is both joyful and a little sad—sad because I am missing out on such a crucial time in his life. But joyful because I get to spend forty-five minutes with him. Based on previous visits, I know his visit will affect my mood for the entire next week. If I allow my mind to focus on all the things in his life I'm missing out on, I will be surly and in a bad mood. But if every time I think about the visit, I simply thank God for the opportunity to have seen him, and trust God to keep him safe, the joy of the visit will last at least a week.

Lord, it may have been through glass talking over a phone, but I got to see my boy for forty-five minutes yesterday. Thank You. Thank You for allowing me to see him and help raise him. Please guide me in being a parent from behind these walls.

Set Free from Your Personal Prison

Psalm 142:7: Set me free from my prison, that I may praise your name. Then the righteous will gather about me because of your goodness to me.

These bars and this jail are one type of prison. But almost everyone has their own personal prison. It may be the prison of addiction—drugs, alcohol, money, power, etc. Or it might be a prison of fear, resulting in violence or other destructive behavior. I have seen a lot of people leave this jail, but those who are still a captive in their own personal prison end up coming right back. It doesn't matter if we are on the inside or outside; we still need God to free us from our personal prison in order to live a life of peace. If we have been freed by God, we are truly free and can find peace even if we remain behind these walls.

Also, when one is free, that person also tends to attract other free people to himself/herself, which is really important here in jail where it's so hard to find positive people who can help us in our walk with the Lord.

Even more important than getting out is being freed by Jesus, finding peace, and becoming the men and women we were meant to be.

Jesus, please free me from my addictions and fears. Help me live a life that attracts righteous people who, like me, want to avoid all the BS that exists here in jail. Even though my body is still locked up, I know You can set me free.

Being Faithful When Sentenced

Jeremiah 42:5-6: Then they said to Jeremiah, "May the Lord be a true and faithful witness against us if we do not act in accordance with everything the Lord your God sends you to tell us. Whether it is favorable or unfavorable, we will obey the Lord our God, to whom we are sending you, so that it will go well with us, for we will obey the LORD our God."

Here in County Jail almost everyone is still waiting to be sentenced. Today at both our Sunday morning Bible sturdy and the afternoon Catholic service, there were prayers for people to be granted a Romero (California has a 3-strikes law and a Romero removes a prior strike from sentencing) and mercy in sentencing. I pray these prayers and hope myself and my brothers are blessed when the time comes, and we will be granted a light sentence. There is of course nothing wrong with praying these prayers and asking God to help us get released as soon as possible. But we must face the possibility that like some faithful brothers who prayed these prayers before us, we may receive a harsh sentence. If that happens, or we do not receive parole, we cannot think God has given up on us or isn't real. *When we have true faith and trust in God we must be willing to obey and follow God regardless when news is favorable or unfavorable.* God is the God of freedom on the outside, but he is also the God of prisons. In the eight months

I have been here I have seen examples of both people who have followed God and continued to trust Him despite a long sentence, and seen some turn away. Those who have accepted their sentence with hope and faith are a great testimony to myself and others around them. I hope when the time comes I too will be able to accept whatever my sentence is with grace and dignity.

Lord I pray for those going to sentencing, and for myself when the day comes. We ask, Lord, that the courts will see our hearts and grant us mercy. But more than even that, please help us to follow You no matter what happens. Be with us and strengthen us no matter what the verdict.

Moving On

2 Samuel 12:22-23: He answered, "While the child was still alive, I fasted and wept. I thought, 'Who knows? The LORD may be gracious to me and let the child live.' But now that he is dead, why should I go on fasting? Can I bring him back again? I will go to him, but he will not return to me."

King David was told his son, who was born to him through Bathsheba with whom he had an affair, was going to die. David fasted and prayed hoping God would change his mind and allow his son to live. When his son eventually does die, his servants are afraid to tell the King, thinking he will sink further into depression, and maybe do something rash and destructive. But once he hears the news his son has died, David stops fasting and resumes his life. He has learned a painful lesson, but also realizes there is no longer a need to fast or think about what happened.

A lot of time we plead with the Lord to do something, to make something happen, like a good outcome with our case, or for a favorable parole hearing, but what do we do when it doesn't go our way? The temptation of many of us is to feel betrayed by God, and we continue to dwell on the outcome. But what good comes from that? Can we change what has already happened? Don't get me wrong. If there are chances for appeal, we should take what we learned and proceed. But, like David, we often should ask ourselves, "How has this thing occurred? How do I take the lessons learned and move on?" We don't want to be like the people in jail who continually rehash a case that has already been decided and curse their luck and spread negativity, always talking about how everyone and everything is against them. They only bring themselves down and all those around them.

At some point we need to move on. Rather than dwell in the past, it's better to live in the present, and just focus on doing the next right thing.

God, grant me the serenity to accept the things I cannot change, courage to change the things I can, and wisdom to know the difference.

God Will Show You a New Way

Isaiah 42:16: "Here is my servant, whom I uphold, my chosen one in whom I delight; I will put my Spirit on him, and he will bring justice to the nations.

As scary as being in prison is, getting out can also be scary, particularly, if one is used to doing the wrong thing. I know from talking to inmates who have gotten out and returned here to County Jail, that some are scared of getting out and coming right back again. They are scared once they face life's challenges that they will go back to drugs. They are scared they won't have enough money, so they will go back to robbery or burglary. They are scared they may get punked, and won't be able to walk away from a fight.

Starting a clean, healthy life on the outside will not be easy for most of us, but God is here to help us if we let Him. We may have been blind in our old ways, but God will show us a better path. This may start with finding healthy relationships with people who are clean and try to do the right thing. AA/NA and churches are some of the easiest ways to get started in this direction. God is reaching out to us and will not forsake us. Asking Him to send positive people into our lives may be the best way to get started and on a better path, even while we are locked up. When we are released, we will need to ask Him again to send positive people into our lives. Joining a church or support group is one of the best ways to help start our new lives on the outside.

"God, thank You. You are showing me a new way to live. Changing my ways is at times scary. Please bring people into my life—here in prison and when I get out—to help me along the way."

Jesus Is the Miracle

John 5:5-9: One who was there had been an invalid for thirty-eight years. When Jesus saw him lying there and learned that he had been in this condition for a long time, he asked him, "Do you want to get well?" "Sir," the invalid replied, "I have no one to help me into the pool when the water is stirred. While I am trying to get in, someone else goes down ahead of me." Then Jesus said to him, "Get up! Pick up your mat and walk." At once the man was cured; he picked up his mat and walked. The day on which this took place was a Sabbath.

Everyone has pain and hurt in their life that they need to be healed from. Too often we wait around hoping that something will come along and miraculously cure us. The cure we are looking for may be from past pain in our lives; it may be from addiction, or it may be a longing for some purpose or better life. We may spend years waiting by a pool of self-help, or at following the latest fads to bring meaning to our lives. Often, we think we just need to find the right girl, or friends, join the right group, or make enough money to fill the hole in our hearts. But Jesus is the answer. He is the one who can heal us. And, it's simpler than we imagine. He only asks us to have the faith and to take that first step and start walking. If you have been looking for happiness in money or drugs and that path has led you to prison, you can be sure that's the wrong path. But Jesus can heal you if you will let him. He is standing there calling. We only need to pick up our mat and walk.

"Jesus, I know that I have been waiting for a "miracle" to make my life better for too long. I now realize You are the miracle I have been searching for. Please come into my life and change me. Become the Lord of my life and help me to pick up my mat and begin to walk with You."

Boasting About Tomorrow

Proverbs 27:1: Do not boast about tomorrow,
for you do not know what a day may bring.

I remember vividly a conversation I once had with my mother. My wife had separated from me and was throwing me out of my own house, and among other things, told me I drink too much. I defended myself telling my mother how successful I was, and how I had everything under control, and I was going to be better without my wife. I was "boasting about tomorrow" instead of taking what my wife was saying as a warning and checking my behavior. Within thirty days of this conversation with my mother, I was arrested due to an alcohol related accident.

I thought I was in control, but in fact, my life was spiraling out of control. I missed the chance to make changes, and now I am paying the price for it, as well as having hurt many people. Sometimes, like in my case, our actions cause lives to tragically change. The point is, we need to always be grateful for what we have and take every opportunity to improve ourselves before it's too late. In jail I started to attend AA and found recovery. If I had the courage to go to meetings earlier, I could have avoided a tragedy.

God, help me not to think I have everything under control and can change my ways later. Help me to see every moment and day is precious, and I always need to take the opportunity to look for ways to improve myself.

Small Blessings

Colossians 3:15: Let the peace of Christ rule in your hearts, since as members of one body you were called to peace. And be thankful.

It's 6:30 a.m. and we just had count and the POD is quiet. My cell is the only one with its light on; everyone else has gone back to sleep and turned their lights off. But sorry, bunkie, mine is on so I can read and write. In the quiet, I experience a rare treat. The deputy is listening to music at his station, and I can hear it. I haven't listened to the radio or heard an actual song for over eleven months. My mind, as it always does, was wandering and thinking about my day ahead—people I will talk to, what I will order on commissary, etc. But I try to stop my mind from wandering. Instead I sit quietly and just listen to the music. If I let my mind wander, I will miss this opportunity. So I just sit and take the music in and enjoy it. Even though jail and prison are hard, God sends us beautiful moments—but sometimes we are too busy to notice them. These moments can be meaningful—a kind word, an act of kindness or generosity, or something really simple like hearing a favorite song on the radio for the first time in over a year. God delights in us and wants us to be delighted by the world. Life here is hard, but it is broken up by small moments of laughter and joy. God sends us these moments, but we must be present to notice them.

Lord thank You for small daily reminders of Your love. Thank You for small unexpected treats. Please help me to notice them when they occur, and help me to stop and rest in them.

Foreigner in Prison

I Peter 1:17: Since you call on a Father who judges each person's work impartially, live out your time as foreigners here in reverent fear.

When I first went to jail I stood out like a sore thumb. I was unfamiliar with jail lingo, and it was pretty obvious I was a fish out of water. I remember my second day being asked if I was a wood, and asking back "What's a wood?" At first some inmates thought I might be an informant, but then they realized I couldn't be because they would never plant an informant who knew so little about jail life. I felt very much like I was in a foreign land.

But that's true for all those who seek God behind bars. We have a higher calling. We have standards of fairness, respect, and a code of living differently than most, and while we must pay the consequences of our crimes, God has forgiven us of our sins. This allows us to be transformed and allows us to live differently than most inmates. We are able to experience the peace and joy that comes from being a child of God. We have a God who transforms us and allows us to become the people we were intended to be. Our code is than different than those around us. We truly are foreigners in a strange land.

God thank You for changing me. Even though I am a foreigner here, please keep me safe and allow others to see the peace and joy that You give me.

Yes, Lord

John 10:3: The gatekeeper opens the gate for him, and the sheep listen to his voice. He calls his own sheep by name and leads them out.

When you call my name,
Yes, Lord.

When you invite me into your presence,
Yes, Lord.

When I am hungry and you feed me,
Yes, Lord.

When I am thirsty and you offer me living water,
Yes, Lord.

When I need to turn the other cheek,
Yes, Lord.

When you offer to forgive me,
Yes, Lord.

To your healing power,
Yes, Lord.

Angels in Jail

Mark 1:12-13: At once the Spirit sent him out into the wilderness, and he was in the wilderness forty days, being tempted by Satan. He was with the wild animals, and angels attended him.

These verses refer to Jesus being tempted by Satan before he started his ministry. But, when I read them, I thought about my experience here in the "wilderness" of prison and of all the "angels" who have attended me. While there are no wild animals here, there are some violent men. But I can also say there are also angels here. There are people who have come into my life to nourish me both physically and spiritually. There have been times when I needed an encouraging word, and I received it through a fellow inmate. A couple months ago, someone came in to lead a Bible Study and during their testimony, they talked about how when they were young and in Mexico, someone killed their father. Initially, this led them down a dark path, but eventually it triggered events that led them to the US, and more importantly, to Christ. I stayed behind to share with this brother the reason I am here; it's because I was in an accident that killed someone's father. As I told him my story, I wept, and he prayed for me. He forgave me on behalf of a person whose father had been killed. This prayer sustained me for many months through a dark time of guilt and shame.

Lord, thank You for sending angels here in jail to minister to me. Many people, including fellow inmates, have been used by

You to help sustain me and get me through this time. Help me to gather the strength to one day repay this kindness by being an "angel" to someone here.

Work for Jesus from Where You Are Now

Luke 8:38-39: The man from whom the demons had gone out begged to go with him, but Jesus sent him away, saying, return home and tell how much God has done for you." So the man went away and told all over town how much Jesus had done for him.

T he man in this verse was possessed by many demons. He lived without clothes in a graveyard. The Bible says people would chain him up to try and keep him under control But, with the demon's power, he would break the chains. When Jesus approached the man the demons recognized him as the Son of God. Jesus commanded those demons to leave the man. The people couldn't believe what they were seeing and were afraid when they saw the man fully clothed and talking calmly with Jesus. The man then wants to go with Jesus, but Jesus tells him to stay and tell everyone what God has done for him.

When God heals us of our demons, figurative or literal, we may want to immediately go and do something "big" in His name— go on a mission field perhaps. God sometimes calls people to do things like that, but you may find such doors don't open for you. You may dream of going out and telling the world of what God has done for you, but like me, you may be in jail or prison so cannot. What Jesus is telling us here is not to wait until we get out to start to work for Him. He is telling us to start now and tell others in our "prison home" what He has done for us.

"Lord, thank You for all You have taught me and all You have healed me from while I have been here in jail. While You can bless me and use me to do Your work when I get out, help me to start now. Help me to be bold in my faith and tell everyone of the great things You have done for me and how You have healed me."

A New Person

Ephesians 4:24: and to put on the new self, created to be like God in true righteousness and holiness.

In County I was celled for a couple months with a young man (25 years old) named Juan (not his real name). Juan had found the Lord while in jail and radiated Christ's love. He still struggled occasionally but he was almost always smiling and eager to help people when he could. One day, Juan showed me newspaper clippings from when he was arrested, and told me about his life before being arrested. The clippings talked about shootings, attempting to harm police, and other acts of violence. I simply said, "I don't know that person. The Juan I know is someone different. You have put on a new self, and you are someone I see as righteous, peaceful, even holy."

God has the power to change everyone. Those of us who have been to prison understand this better than most. We all know people like Juan. People who were once to be feared, but now have been transformed by the love of Jesus. Juan will be in prison for at least another nine years, but he is living a changed and peaceful life.

"Lord, thank you for Juan and all he has taught me. Please change me. Help me to experience Your love in such a way I am unrecognizable to many who knew me in my old life and ways. Help me to put on Your righteousness, and help me to never judge people based on their past, but know Your power can create something beautiful in all of us."

Feeling Like Your Spirit Is Crushed

Psalm 34:18: The Lord is close to the broken-hearted and saves those who are crushed in spirit.

Today my pastor visited me. I was trying to relate to him how it has been for me lately. I feel worn out. I had thought my case would have been settled a long time ago. I've been here over a year and I have another four to five months before I will be sentenced. This past week was both my birthday and my son's, but because someone visited me unexpectedly, my visits were used up, and I didn't get to see him. I also had the flu this past week. I feel drained physically, emotionally, and spiritually. Then while I was telling my pastor all this, two deputies walked in and served me with new lawsuit papers. Sometimes I feel like it is too much. I feel like I cannot take it anymore; I feel like I have reached a breaking point. At times like this I have no clarity. I do not know my future, and it feels hopeless. At these times I have to trust the Lord. Although I can't always feel or sense His presence, I know that He is near. I know He will sustain me; I know I just need to hang on and soon He will refresh my soul.

"Lord, I am crushed and my spirit and will are broken. My future appears bleak. All I seem to get is bad news, but I know You are near. I know You will never leave me. Please make Your presence felt and give me faith to know You are always looking out for me, regardless of how I feel in the moment."

Our Own Path

John 21:21-22: When Peter saw him, he asked, "Lord, what about him?" Jesus answered, "If I want him to remain alive until I return, what is that to you? You must follow me."

I am in County Jail awaiting sentencing. One by one, fellow believers go before the judge to be sentenced. We always pray for them and assure each other we need to have faith when we pray for mercy from the courts. Sometimes someone will come back from court "Blessed." They've been spared a prison sentence and instead sent to a recovery program. Whenever this happens, inevitably they will say, "You just have to have faith." Someone will chime in, "That's right, if we have enough faith we can move mountains. God will grant you a program if you have enough faith."

God does have the power to influence your case and have the judge and DA more sympathetic to you, which may result in you getting a program instead of prison time. But Jesus reminds Peter we all have different paths. Some will receive an acquittal, some a program, and some of us will go to prison.

Your sentencing is not a test of God's power. *It is a test of each of us to see if we trust God regardless of the verdict.* He has chosen different paths for each of us. Follow yours. Follow Him. No matter what the path before you.

"Lord, as I write this I still do not know which "sentencing path" You will send me down. I hope it's not prison. But help me

to accept whatever it is. Please deepen my faith no matter what happens. Teach me I can trust You no matter where I am at."

Remember the Lessons of Jail

Deuteronomy 6:12: be careful that you do not forget the Lord, who brought you out of Egypt, out of the land of slavery.

The experience of being arrested and put in jail has changed me in many positive ways. I think I am much more patient. I understand people I never did before, and I've learned many lessons about relying on the Lord's grace and mercy. In addition, I've become much closer to my family and those people who have supported me and stood by me, despite my public failing. I've also had to confront my lifestyle of drinking and understand the effects it had on me and my family. These are all important things I have learned and have the potential to make me a better person, father, and friend when I get out.

That is, if in fact, I remember and adhere to these lessons. One of my biggest fears is that these lessons don't stay with me. In my time here, I have seen many inmates leaving, sounding sincere, and vowing to change their ways, but it's only a matter of months before they return.

It's easy to criticize the Israelites for their lack of faith. One day they witness God's awesome power and see the Red Sea parted. Very shortly thereafter, they think God is going to let them die in the desert. It seems silly they lose faith so quickly, but we are often the same way. When we get back to the struggles and temptations of the outside world, too many of us forget all that God did for us here on the inside.

"Lord, please use this time to grow me spiritually and please use me while I am here. But, also, prepare me to leave. Help me never forget how I relied on You while I was here, and how You continually protected and nourished me."

His Will No Matter Where

Luke 22:42: Father, if you are willing, take this
cup from me; yet not my will, but yours be done."

Once we find Jesus, are we willing to give up everything for Him and for our spiritual growth? What if
we found the perfect place to get to know Him and it
was in jail—would we be willing to do more time? As I sit in
County Jail awaiting trial, this is a question I struggle with. I
want to be out so badly, but if it's God's will or part of a bigger
plan, am I willing to be here and stay in jail or go to prison to
do His will?

Am I able, like Jesus in the garden, to be able to say, "Not my
will but thine be done?" I know there is work to be done for
the kingdom both here and on the outside. I want to be in His
will. But of course, I cannot truly know His plans. So while I
will do everything in my power to get out of here and be with
my family, I must also accept His direction wherever I am. So
today it's here in County Jail. In three months it may be here,
be on the outside, or in San Quentin. The key is—no matter
where I am to keep looking to Him and doing all I can to serve
Him, knowing I am loved and protected by Him.

*"Lord, You know how badly I want and pray for the gift of
mercy from the Judge so that I can rejoin my boys on the outside and resume my life. But wherever the next phase of my
journey leads, help me to praise You, be grateful for all You
have done for me, and have an attitude of service to You."*

Morning Is Coming

Psalm 30:5: For his anger lasts only a moment, but his favor lasts a lifetime; weeping may stay for the night, but rejoicing comes in the morning.

I know that if I trust the Lord and learn the lessons He has for me through my jail experience, I can emerge from here as a better person. This period in my life is "the night." I spend time here in sorrow and "weeping," mostly for the opportunities and time with my family I am missing out on. But I am also confident that when I do get out, I will no longer take time with my boys for granted. I plan on relishing every moment I get to spend with them. I am also hopeful I will be a far more patient person than I was in the past. I now miss the little things that irritated me in the past. I long to stand in the grocery line, wait for a slow internet connection, or miss a turn and have to drive around the block. I cannot imagine I will ever complain again that my coffee is too cold or hot. (It's always lukewarm when I make it from the sink here.) Yes, I will appreciate showers, cooking, having a pen, being able to text people, mowing the lawn, going to the bathroom in private—this is the night, but the morning I get out I will rejoice in the ordinary things of life.

"Lord, being in jail has taught me how much I took life for granted, and how much I have to be grateful for. Please let this be a lesson I never forget when I am free from these walls."

Being Pruned for Good

John 15:1-2: "I am the true vine, and my Father is the gardener. He cuts off every branch in me that bears no fruit, while every branch that does bear fruit he prunes so that it will be even more fruitful.

I am in County Jail awaiting trial and just had a visit from my lawyer. As often seems to be the case, he brought more bad news about my situation. Seeking comfort, I thumbed through my Bible and came across these verses.

Before I was arrested, I was a Christian and regularly attended church and was part of a morning men's group. And even though I was sincere in my faith, and tried to do the right thing, I was headed down a dark path. I had recently separated from my wife and was drinking too much. While I still tried to do what was best in the sight of God and my family, I certainly wasn't bearing much fruit. I was trapped in a bad cycle and things were probably going to get worse. Then I was in the accident that brought me here. As I sit here awaiting trial, I often pray for a favorable outcome. And occasionally it seems there are reasons to be optimistic. But, like I mentioned earlier, inevitably the optimism fades to the stark reality of my situation. While this time in jail is stressful, it does not have to be wasted. And I can't help but wonder if God is pruning me through this time here. There is certainly an opportunity to learn from this time and become more fruitful than I would be if I had never come to jail. Since there are other people involved, I can never say what happened was worth it, but I do know that if I allow Him, God can use this time to prune me and make me into a better person.

"Lord, I am troubled and afraid, worried about my future and how much time I may have to spend in prison. However much time it is, use this time to prune me, shape me into the person I can be, help me to live for You and love those around me here, now, and prepare me for the day I eventually get out."

The Three Questions

Philippians 4:11-1:3: I am not saying this because I am in need, for I have learned to be content whatever the circumstances. I know what it is to be in need, and I know what it is to have plenty. I have learned the secret of being content in any and every situation, whether well fed or hungry, whether living in plenty or in want. I can do all this through him who gives me strength.

I recently talked on the phone with someone who was completely miserable. The circumstances in her life suddenly changed and she blames others and lashes out at everyone. Later, I realized that even though I am in jail, I am happier and more content with my life than she is with hers—even though I'm stuck behind bars and she is free. Victor Frankel, survivor of a Nazi Concentration camp, wrote, "Our last freedom is to choose our attitude despite our circumstances." I'm in jail. I don't pretend to be happy about that, or enjoy it, but I shape my attitude by trying to focus on three questions every day.

First: What am I grateful for? Every day I try to list up to ten things I am grateful for despite being in jail. Some of the same things I list are small mercies and blessings that happen here. Almost always on my list is the health of my family on the outside. Focusing on the positive and what I am grateful for is essential for my well-being while I am here. Having an attitude of gratitude keeps the darkness of jail from consuming me.

Second: What is the lesson? God is always prodding us, teaching us. There are lessons to be learned every day. The trick is to focus our attention on these lessons and learn from them, instead of letting them pass us by. If we are learning and growing our time, even jail time, is not wasted.

Third: Given where I am at this moment, what is the next right thing to do? Instead of worrying about what I should do in years to come, I focus on the next thing, and let the future take care of itself. It's hard to know what we should be doing in five or ten years. But it's easy to know the right thing to do in the next fifteen minutes. And usually the answer to that question is we simply need to love the person in front of us

When I focus on these questions, my attitude is better and my spirits are lifted. I am free, even in jail.

"Lord, despite my circumstances, You've blessed me. Thank You. Help me to have a grateful heart, and help me to see and appreciate the lessons You are giving me today. And while it may be hard to always do the right thing, help me to do the next right thing put before me."

Get Moving

Exodus 14:15: Then the Lord said to Moses, "Why are you crying out to me?' Tell the people to move on.

S ometimes we just need to get moving. We have prayed. We have prepared ourselves. But sometimes we just get stuck. Here in jail I recently found myself in a rut. Sometimes I feel like my world is so small and so little changes. I become bored and complacent. I know the things I could and should do, but I become lethargic. I'm not talking about taking a healthy break. I'm talking about sometimes I would rather sit in my cell and just play Sudoku all day than engage with anyone or do any of the things to improve myself or teach myself something. Again, there is nothing wrong with taking a break, but when I become stuck I know the answer— the answer is simply to get moving—talk to that person I've been meaning to—start reading that book—sign up for a class—make the call—write the letter—just take a step forward. Stop complaining to God about all the reasons I can't or don't want to and just take action! Once the first step is taken, the next is so much easier and before you know it you are on your way.

"Lord, show me where I need to take action today. Reveal to me an area of my life that I have been procrastinating in and need to stop complaining and just get moving."

Christian Brothers

Psalm 119:63: I am a friend to all who fear you, to all who follow your precepts.

Here in the pod I am in in County Jail, we recently received a large influx of new inmates. It's always good to see some of them at our Bible Study on Sundays. No matter our different backgrounds, race, or paths in life, I always feel a special bond with other Christians. So I seek out these brothers and try to get to know them and encourage them. In return, I am often encouraged and able to learn from them. While we certainly are not perfect, (we are in jail, after all), I know if they are brothers in Christ we have a special bond and can rely on each other. These are the men God has sent to help me get through this. I am not naïve. I know a lot of inmates come to church for different reasons, but I also know that it has been here at church in jail that I have found fellow believers who are helping me navigate this part of my journey. I don't know how I would make it through these days without these brothers.

"God, thank You that even though I am here in jail I am not alone. Not only are You with me, but there are also Christian brothers here. Please help us to find each other and use us to strengthen and encourage each other."

God is There When We Are Slipping

Psalm 94:18-19: When I said, "My foot is slipping," your unfailing love, Lord, supported me. When anxiety was great within me, your consolation brought me joy.

Recently I accepted a plea deal in my case and I now await sentencing. Going to court and admitting to what I was accused of was incredibly difficult. For the past year, for legal reasons, I did not admit to anything. But now, in open court, I heard horrible charges read, and I pled no contest to them. The process was incredibly difficult for me. I truly have "slipped," and have had to rely on the unfailing love of the Lord to support me. In the courtroom my anxiety level was very high, and for a moment I even thought I might faint. But through it all, I have been learning about God and his great love for me. I know that God sent his Son to die for me knowing one day I would be in a courtroom guilty of terrible sins. When I think that he knows everything about me and loves me anyway, it brings me great comfort.

I am lucky I have parents who model this behavior as well. Despite what I've done, they have stood by me and supported me every step of the way, driving an hour and a half each way to visit me for forty-five minutes every other week. The love of God and my family has truly given me the comfort I need to survive this experience. Even if you don't have friends or family, God is there to wrap his arms around you.

"Lord, thank You for being with me through this experience. Thank You for helping to relieve my anxiety by showing me You will stay with me wherever I go—whether it's home, or through the gates of San Quentin."

Being Content

Psalm 131:1-3: My heart is not proud, Lord, my eyes are not haughty; I do not concern myself with great matters or things too wonderful for me. But I have calmed and quieted myself, I am like a weaned child with its mother; like a weaned child I am content. Israel, put your hope in the Lord both now and forevermore.

Before I was arrested, I often wondered about "The Great Mysteries of the Universe." Why is there suffering in the world? Why do bad things happen to good people? How did God create the universe, etc., etc. Then when I was first arrested, I used to wonder why was I where I was when my accident happened? What would my life be like now if I hadn't been arrested? And sometimes my mind would go on and on like that and drive me crazy. But I know I will never know the answers to such questions.

While I will never know the answers to those "great mysteries" I liked to ponder and discuss with my friends. I'm also now at the point where I am ok with not knowing. Now that so much of my life has been taken from me, now that my future is so uncertain, now that I no longer have security or money or a prestigious career, all I can do is sit and trust God. I am quieter now. I only want to know that I am loved, and that God hasn't forsaken me. I want to sit with Him like a young child sits with his father and be slowly rocked to sleep, content and safe in His arms.

"Lord, help me to realize and completely understand You are all I have ever needed."

Man Up

1 Corinthians 13:11: When I was a child, I talked like a child, I thought like a child, I reasoned like a child. When I became a man, I put the ways of childhood behind me."

Now that we have time to reflect, many of us convicts look back on our lives and see how selfish and immature we were. We now realize how our immature and childish actions got us locked up. Petty disagreements or arguments may have escalated to violence, and now we may face years in prison. Or maybe demanding your way like a selfish child led to your getting locked up. No matter what got us to prison, many of us now realize it's time to "man up." It's time to man up, and be a father to our sons and daughters. It's time to man up and be the husband or boyfriend women expect us to be. It's time to man up and get clean and sober for once and all, and stop the cycle of drugs and alcohol that leads to prison. It's time to man up and get a job, even if the job isn't exactly what we want or pays as much as drug dealing or stealing. Lots of prisoners talk about "manning up" while they are locked up, but go right back to their ways as soon as they leave prison gates. Don't do that.

"Lord, help me to begin to man up and take responsibility for my life. Show me how to become a responsible person and live like you want me to and break this prison cycle."

Some Good Can Come Through Suffering

Psalm 119:71: It was good for me to be afflicted so that I might learn your decrees.

I've heard many people here in jail say they weren't as much arrested as they were rescued. Being arrested gave them a chance to look at how they were living and for many to get clean. Also, for many of us, our time in prison allows us to get closer to God. We have time to reflect on our lives and behavior. We have time to read the Bible and pray. Further, we are desperate and stripped of our ego that thinks we can solve our problems on our own. So we turn to God. There is nothing wrong with this. Sometimes it's only in pain and our aloneness that we turn to God. In this way, many of us gain through our time in prison. We come to better understand God, and turn our lives completely over to him. In these cases, it benefits us to go to jail. In our "affliction," we learn about God and reset our lives while we are here, and when we get out we can become the men that God, our families, and we ourselves want us to be. Sometimes we need to thank God for loving us enough to let us get arrested.

"Lord, thank You for using this time for my benefit. While I wish I hadn't had to come to jail; please help me to never forget the lessons I have learned here so this time is not wasted."

God Makes Us New

Isaiah 43:18-19: "Forget the former things; do not dwell on the past. See, I am doing a new thing! Now it springs up; do you not perceive it? I am making a way in the wilderness and streams in the wasteland.

For some reason, sometimes we want to hold on to the past, even though doing so is usually destructive. It's true we need to remember the lessons of our past, and we learn and grown from these lessons. But too often we glamorize a destructive past and think somehow we can do things still do the things that got us into trouble but next time the results will be different. Here in jail at the AA and NA meetings we often refer to this as the definition of insanity—doing the same thing but somehow expecting different results.

We need to "forget" our sinful natures that brought us to this point in our lives. We are new creatures in Christ and no longer under the bondage of sin. There is no reason to dwell on the past. We must forgive ourselves, make amends when possible, and allow God to change us. He wants to do something new with us—something exciting that will give us peace, joy, and a new purpose. Sometimes change in us occurs slowly, and we might not notice it.

Recently, a couple of people commented to me they appreciated how I carry myself here in jail. I hadn't even noticed I was doing anything different, but I often notice it in my Christian brothers here. When we show Christ's love to others in prison we stand out like "streams in a wasteland."

"Lord, help me to forget my sinful desires; change me so I thirst for You. Help me to show love to others here in jail. Help me to be a stream in the wasteland."

God Doesn't Forget Us

Isaiah 49:15-16: "Can a mother forget the baby at her breast and have no compassion on the child she has borne? Though she may forget, I will not forget you! See, I have engraved you on the palms of my hands; your walls are ever before me.

When I first came to jail I received a lot of mail. I was lucky so many friends and family wanted to stay in touch, see how I was doing, and make sure I was ok. But I've now been here for over a year. At this point only a couple very close and faithful friends and family members still write. While I'm sure the rest haven't completely forgotten about me, I am out of sight and out of mind. To be honest, at times I feel alone and forgotten. Sometimes when I do get letters from people they say they will visit soon or put money on my books. But usually they don't. I've actually learned not to expect too much. I'm sure these friends have the best of intentions, but as they go about their busy lives, they forget about me.

But God doesn't forget about us. Even though at times it may seem like we are alone, He is here with us. He is walking beside us and willing to help us when we ask. He promises to stay with us and remember us no matter what we've done or where we go. He is Lord not only on the outside but also here behind these walls. He constantly reminds me of His presence through my Bible readings, and sometimes through an encouraging word from a fellow inmate. Our names are tattooed on His hands.

"Lord, thank You that while others who have once supported me seem to have forgotten me, You never will. Thank You I am Your son, and You will never forsake me. Help me to never forget others who will be here after I get out. Help me to continue to demonstrate Your love to them."

Don't Get Caught Up in Busyness

Luke 10:39-42: She had a sister called Mary, who sat at the Lord's feet listening to what he said. But Martha was distracted by all the preparations that had to be made. She came to him and asked, "Lord, don't you care that my sister has left me to do the work by myself? Tell her to help me!" "Martha, Martha," the Lord answered, "you are worried and upset about many things, but few things are needed—or indeed only one. Mary has chosen what is better, and it will not be taken away from her."

It seems there is always lot to do. When we are busy, it's easy to lose sight of what's really important, even when we are busy doing good or positive things. For example, of course, reading the Bible and Christian books are a good thing. But sometimes I can get so caught up in just getting through my daily readings. I don't focus on truly experiencing God. It was through the writings of Richard Roar that I came to realize it's not about spiritual perfection; it's about spiritual union.

For example, I have a goal of reading ten chapters a day out of the Bible. There is nothing wrong with that, except, there are times I get so caught up in meeting that goal, I don't take the time to understand what I read. If reading less would mean I would learn more, I should read less. And sometimes I become so fixated on ensuring I bring everyone on my prayer checklist to God, I quickly mumble through their names and don't truly lift them to the Lord. I am often so busy getting through my devotions I don't spend any time listening to God. Bible reading, reading Christian books, and prayer are of course, a key to knowing God. But even these can distract us from experiencing God. It's never about the number of chapters we read or minutes we spend in prayer; it's about "sitting at the Lord's feet and listening to what He says."

"Lord, please help me to be more like Mary and choose to really listen to You. Help me to experience and really feel Your love. Please don't let me be fooled by just going through the motions of spiritual practices."

What Quenches Your Thirst?

John 4:13-14: Jesus answered, "Everyone who drinks this water will be thirsty again, but whoever drinks the water I give them will never thirst. Indeed, the water I give them will become in them a spring of water welling up to eternal life."

When we were on the streets, most of us looked to money, drugs, alcohol, sex, or power to make us happy. These things make us feel happy for a brief time, but they never really satisfy us. Instead they push us to keep trying to get "more." Any drug addict can tell you this. While their lives crumbled around them, their bodies kept telling them simply to get more drugs, no matter what the risk or potential consequences. This is, of course, why so many people are in jail for drug-related offenses or crimes to get money for drugs. When we look to be satisfied with this "water" we will only thirst again. Jesus, and God's love is the only thing that can truly satisfy us. We all have a longing within us, a search for a purpose, that we can either run from by using drugs or any other worldly substitute, or we can submit to God and His will. When we do stop running and submit for the first time, we taste the water we have been searching for. This is the living water that Jesus promises us.

"Jesus, please fill me with your spirit—which is the living water I truly want and need. Only You can grant me real satisfaction and peace. Forgive me for having searched for fulfillment in worldly pleasures, and heal me with Your living water."

No Fear of Bad News

Psalm 112:6-8: Surely the righteous will never be shaken; they will be remembered forever. They will have no fear of bad news; their hearts are steadfast, trusting in the Lord. Their hearts are secure; they will have no fear; in the end they will look in triumph on their foes.

Before I was arrested, this was a favorite verse of mine. I took comfort in the fact that no matter how bad things might seem, surely there were brighter days ahead. If God was on my side, how bad could things really be? Well, this has been really put to the test for me now that I am in jail. Now I know new levels of how bad things can get. I am still awaiting sentencing which, of course, could bring really bad, even devastating news. But I've already written about fellow brothers who have faced "bad sentencing news" with grace and dignity knowing God is in control. So I think about that and try to have the same attitude. I also think about heaven. If I truly understand what it meant to live for eternity with God, I know my perspective would change. I would realize that years spent in prison are nothing compared to an eternity with God. I try to trust in the Lord, knowing it is better to be "free" in prison than a slave to drugs, alcohol, or money on the outside.

"Lord, help me to truly understand that if I trust You, I can have peace and joy regardless of my circumstances. Show me that You are here with me, and with You by my side, any storm can be weathered. Help me to be brave, trusting You, in the face of bad news."

God Respects Us

Psalm 139:13-14: For you created my inmost being;
you knit me together in my mother's womb. I praise
you because I am fearfully and wonderfully made;
your works are wonderful, I know that full well.

It's easy to get down on yourself when you're behind bars.
Not only are you likely to feel guilty, but others constantly
remind you of your failings. Family may berate you.
Friends may abandon you. Guards constantly remind you of
your lesser status. Yesterday I made the mistake of starting
down stairs when a guard was about to come up, and he pointed
at me and screamed, "Get off the stairs when you see a deputy."
I had to stand and wait for him to pass before I could go down.
It felt completely humiliating. Often when I go to the deputy
station to make a request, they don't even acknowledge me or
look up, leaving me to wonder if they heard me. If I ask again
though, I usually am yelled at, "I heard you!" they snap. All
this is enough to make me feel "less than" if I let it. But while
we may be inmates, and while we have made some serious mistakes, we are not "less than" in God's eyes. God created us and
knew what He was doing when He did so. Nothing we can do
can change His love for us. And nothing we can do can change
the fact that we are "fearfully and wonderfully made."

*"God, thank You for creating me the way You did. Thank You
that You knew me and have always known me. Your works are
wonderful. I am one of Your works and I am wonderful. Please
help me remember that today."*

Being Afraid and in Despair

Psalm 22:1: My God, my God, why have you forsaken me? Why are you so far from saving me, so far from my cries of anguish?

Psalm 69:29: But as for me, afflicted and in pain—may your salvation, God, protect me.

Psalm 69:33: The LORD hears the needy and does not despise his captive people.

"Guilty." My friend just finished his trial. While intoxicated, he had been in a fatal accident. Due to a prior DUI offense, the jury had the option of giving him either manslaughter or second degree murder. Unfortunately, and despite our fervent prayers, they found him guilty of second degree murder, which carries fifteen to life. We have been praying for mercy, and he has been praying and fasting, and still the jury returned a guilty verdict. In times like this, we feel drained and like we have been punched in the stomach. God did not answer our prayers, and now my friend faces a life sentence. At times like this, I have more questions than answers.

But I do take comfort in a couple things. First, when writing the psalms, David is honest about his feelings. When we feel abandoned by God and alone, we can express that to him. It's like a time I remember my son being hurt and afraid when I was talking to him about my pending divorce with his mother. He was sad and couldn't talk. I begged him, "It's ok to be mad at me." Then I said, "Just tell me what you're feeling." So now I am telling God in my prayers how we are disappointed and confused as to why He let this happen. I know He hears us and loves us. We face fear and disappointment and suffering. Why He doesn't relieve those, I do not know. I may never know. But I do know, that He is here and He cares. He is here and beside my friend as he goes through his journey, just as He is here with me, as He is with you.

"Lord, please comfort us in our times of fear and despair. I'm disappointed and afraid, but I know you love me. Please make your presence known to me; Show me your love and help me rest in it."

Ignore the Naysayers

John 5:8-10: Then Jesus said to him, "Get up! Pick up your mat and walk." At once the man was cured; he picked up his mat and walked. The day on which this took place was a Sabbath, and so the Jewish leaders said to the man who had been healed, "It is the Sabbath; the law forbids you to carry your mat."

When a miracle happens to us, we are excited and expect others to be excited too. But for many inmates who change their lives for the better in prison and develop a relationship with Jesus, when they get out, they find out their friends and family may not be happy for them. They may doubt they have really changed or pressure them to return to their old ways. I know many inmates who intended to stay clean and start going to church when they got out. But were met by their "friends" outside the gate with drugs or a 40, and immediately they turned back to their old ways.

If you have experienced a miracle in prison—found or re-found Jesus, don't expect it to be easy when you get out. Many people may dismiss your faith or try to get you to go back to ripping and running. You may need to change your friends and the places where you hang out. Actually, for many, this is a necessity if they want to stay clean. Expect to find opposition and naysayers. But resolve to find new friends and a church family to help you.

"Lord, thank You for the miracle You've done in my life. Don't let me be naive and think I can make it on my own when I get out. Please help me to find supportive family and friends to help me transition to a new way of life on the outside."

Focus on Small Blessings

Psalm 84:6-7: As they pass through the Valley of Baka, they make it a place of springs; the autumn rains also cover it with pools. They go from strength to strength, till each appears before God in Zion.

For many of us, prison is our Valley of Sorrows (this is what Valley of Baka means). But even here, there are blessings to be grateful for: money put on our books by a friend, a visit, a kind word, hearing our loved ones are doing well on the outside, a chance to watch a new movie, a good game on the yard, getting into a class etc. If we focus on these blessings it helps to sustain us despite being in prison—this is what is meant by going strength to strength. I think prison is a raging river, but if we jump from stone to stone—blessing to blessing—we can make it to the other side. This is why I like to make a list every day of things I am grateful for. Making the list keeps me grounded on the goodness of God, and helps me to focus on the positive instead of the negative aspects of our environment. We can trust God to supply enough rocks so we can safely cross the stream and get to the other side.

"Lord, thank You for the many blessings You send me every day. Even though at times this jail can feel overwhelming, I know you are granting me small mercies each day to sustain me. Help me keep an attitude of gratitude today and help me make it to the other side."

Better with Jesus

Psalm 84:10: Better is one day in your courts than a thousand elsewhere; I would rather be a doorkeeper in the house of my God than dwell in the tents of the wicked.

Sometimes I am in a panic about the time I am spending in jail. I came to jail at fifty-one years old. I have a son in college and one in high school. I am missing out on crucial years of their lives. This is also the time of life I should be saving and starting to think about retirement, but instead I have lost all my life savings and will be getting out and having to start over in my fifties. But it's also true for me, and many brothers here with me in jail, that we have renewed our faith and will be much closer to God when we get out. Time spent on the outside living a life apart from God is time more wasted than being in here. Yes, when I get out I will have less time left in life than when I came in, but if I'm truly changed, I will have gained from the experience. If I emerge as a better father, even though I may have less time to spend with my boys before they move out on their own, I can take better advantage of what time I have left. In the same way, I may have less time to "live," but if I spend it living for Jesus, it will more than make up for my time behind bars.

"Lord, thank You that I will eventually get another chance on the outside. Please help make the changes I have committed to become permanent in my life, starting with the rest of my time here and continuing when I get out. Help me to truly live with You in Your dwelling."

Serve God in Little Things

> 2 Kings 5:13: Naaman's servants went to him
> and said, "My father, if the prophet had told you
> to do some great thing, would you not have
> done it? How much more, then, when he tells
> you, 'Wash and be cleansed'!"

In this story, an army general named Naaman went to the
prophet Elisha and asked to be cleansed of his disease of
leprosy. When Elisha tells him to go wash himself in the
Jordan River seven times, he becomes indignant. In this verse,
Naaman's servants point out if Elisha had told him to do something huge or challenging, he would have done it without com-
plaint, so why not do something so easy?

I'm often the same way. If God calls us (and makes it obvious)
to do some huge ministry we are willing, but we find it hard to
simply love the person in front of us. I sometimes say it's easier
to jump in front of a bus to save your wife than it is to do the
dishes. We all want to be heroes, but the heroic thing is to do
the right thing every day, and it's usually something simple and
small—a kind word, helping someone studying for their GED,
inviting someone to a religious service, or maybe sharing commissary, are the type of little things God calls us to do.

Let's start by doing little things we can do now, right here, behind bars, and if God provides us a bigger opportunity later,
we can do that then.

"Lord, please direct and show me today how I can serve You by doing the "little things." Help me not consider any task too small or beneath me. Let me love the person You put in my path today."

Do the Work

1 Chronicles 28:10: Consider now, for the Lord has chosen you to build a house as the sanctuary. Be strong and do the work.

1 Chronicles 28:20: David also said to Solomon his son, "Be strong and courageous, and do the work. Do not be afraid or discouraged, for the Lord God, my God, is with you. He will not fail you or forsake you until all the work for the service of the temple of the Lord is finished.

After King David turned his kingdom over to his son, Solomon, David told his son to do the work God had for him—in his case, build the temple where they would worship God. He told him, "God has chosen you, be strong, be brave, and do the work."

In our own lives, even if we are behind bars, God has a plan for us and work to do. That work may be living as an example to others of God's love. It may be getting clean and sober so when you get out you can be the man God wants you to be. Your work may be repairing relationships that may have been broken before or because of your incarceration. For now, part of my work is writing thoughts about how the Bible speaks to me as someone behind bars, in the hopes it may encourage someone else. I often sit thinking I should write something, but until I actually start putting pen to paper, nothing is accomplished. I need to not procrastinate. I need to simply follow David's call and start getting to work.

Is there something you need to get to work at today?

"Lord, it's easy to just sit in my cell and play cards or do puzzle magazines, but I know there is also work to do. I know You don't want me to burn out or feel guilty if I take an occasional day off, but please help keep me motivated so I can do the work You have set before me."

Don't Do the Minimum

> John 6:28-30: Then they asked him, "What must we do to do the works God requires?" Jesus answered, "The work of God is this: to believe in the one he has sent." So they asked him, "What sign then will you give that we may see it and believe you? What will you do?"

The people in this passage remind me a lot of myself sometimes. First they ask, "What does God require?" Not what would please him, but what does he require? In other words, what is the minimum we need to do for God? They then follow this up with "What will you do?" In other words, what is the minimum I can do for God to get what I want? Too often this is my attitude, and perhaps yours, as we treat God like a vending machine. We put a little good in and expect something in return. I see that a lot in County Jail as most of us await trial or sentencing. Many come to Bible Study or pray hoping God will help them. But once sentenced, they no longer come. This is a mentality focused solely on personal needs. If I do for you, God, what will you do for me?

I also see this same attitude on the outside. Sometimes, we pick a church to go to strictly on how it meets our needs. We do have needs, and should pick a church accordingly, but when we focus solely on our desires and find reasons not to go to a church because the music isn't lively enough, the pastor is boring, or people didn't help me, we are thinking only of ourselves. Our focus should be on God, and how we can be of service.

It's the same thing here in jail; maybe I think the person coming to lead the Bible Study is boring, and I would rather watch a movie or play chess than go. But I should still go as a way to express my gratitude for the person who gave up his time to come into jail and teach us. Plus, my attendance may be an encouragement to others. While it doesn't always happen, I often find even if I don't initially feel like going to a Bible Study or Church service here in jail, I leave encouraged and am glad I went.

"Lord, please give me a heart of gratitude, then I can see the needs of others and help them. Please show me when and where I am too worried about having my own needs met."

Never Give Up

2 Chronicles 15:7 but as for you, be strong and courageous, for your work will be rewarded.

In the program I am in here in County Jail, inmates are encouraged to write back to the pod after they leave and let us know how they are doing—whether they are in prison, a program, or outside. We read these letters at our morning meetings. Recently, we read another letter from Tom. It was Tom's first letter to us as a free man. Although I have never met Tom, I know him from the many letters he has written back to the pod in the year and a half I have been here. Tom came to this pod fifteen years ago facing a life sentence. The information he heard about alcohol and drug abuse as well as how to better relate and respond to other people began to change him. Then he found God and accepted Jesus as his personal Lord and Savior. While Tom changed his life in here, he could not change his past, and he received a life sentence and left this pod for San Quentin. But as he began to serve his life sentence, Tom truly was a changed man. He became involved in ministry in prison as an inmate, attended college, and helped others whenever he could. He received a college degree, then a Master's Degree, and continued to write and update everyone here on his progress. He started at a level four yard, but because of his behavior and attitude kept getting moved to lower level yards and eventually ended up at a fire house. Then after fifteen years was granted early parole.

I know it doesn't happen for everyone, but Tom was strong, never gave up doing the right thing, and was rewarded with early release. We must never give up or lose hope.

"Lord, help me to stay strong. Help me to never give up working for You, and doing the right thing. Sometimes I am discouraged, but please remind me, my efforts are not in vain."

Marking Time

Psalm 90:12: Teach us to number our days, that
we may gain a heart of wisdom.

I recently began the one-year countdown to my release date.
Your release date may be a long way off, but time has a
way of passing and hopefully you are there before you realize it. A lot of inmates I've talked to have different ways of
counting down their remaining time. Some with a lot of years
count birthdays or holidays only. Others with less time count
Fridays or laundry days as a way of marking their time. I've
decided to count down twenty-six, two-week increments. That
way I can establish two-week goals and have enough time to
make these goals both meaningful and achievable.

But I can't think of a better goal for my remaining time than
the one in today's verse, "That I may gain a heart of wisdom."
If there is one thing most of us have in prison, it's time. We can
use that time to study, to think, to pray, to learn everything we
can about God, and to obtain a heart of wisdom. Will you join
me in dedicating your remaining time to learning everything
you can about God, and obtaining wisdom that will carry over
into your life on the outside?

"Lord, please take my remaining time and use it to be of ser-
vice to You right here behind these bars. Help me to reflect
Your love and demonstrate it daily. Also, please teach me more
about You. Let me learn as much about You as possible while
I have this time I can use to study without all the distractions
that will be there when I eventually get out."

It's Not Who You Know

Acts 19:15: One day the evil spirit answered them, "Jesus I know, and Paul I know about, but who are you?"

Sometimes in our Bible Studies here in jail, people will say, "I used to go to a great church" or "My parents were really spiritual" or "I knew this one guy who was a really great Christian." Sometimes I find myself doing this as well. If someone comes in from a church where I know people, I'll ask them if they know such and such. I guess I'm trying to impress them by showing who I know.

There is an old saying, "God has no grandchildren." In other words, God isn't impressed by who we know or how spiritual our parents or grandparents were. He wants to know us only through Jesus, not through other people. Yes, we need spiritual teachers and guides to help us, but ultimately we each need to come to God and ask Him to reveal himself to us. This can be done through prayer and reading of the Bible. Let's not rely on our connections. Let's go to God directly, and ask Him to heal us and help us change things we need to change.

"God, thank You that I do not have to know the right people in order to be introduced to You. Thank You that I can come to You directly. Please bless me by revealing Yourself to me through Your Word and Holy Sprint that I might know You personally."

Witness Through Actions

Hebrews 12:14: Make every effort to live in peace with everyone and to be holy; without holiness no one will see the Lord.

I am often surprised at how much fellow inmates know about the Bible. I've heard many inmates quote numerous verses in Bible Study or instantly know the chapter and verse when someone quotes a small part of a passage. I, myself, attended a Christian College for a short time, and consider myself fairly knowledgeable about the Bible. But it's not about what we know, it's about how we act. Obviously, our knowledge did not keep us from being sent to jail!

This is especially true in being a witness to others. St. Francis once said, "Preach Jesus always, and if you have to, use words." Rarely would a person want to follow our God if we preach one thing, and then act another way on the yard.

In this passage Paul tells us to be holy. He says if we are not holy, no one will see the Lord. He's right, because those around us know Jesus not by what we say, but by what we do. If we want to be witnesses for Christ, we should first check how we act. Do we show respect to others? Despite our circumstances, do we show love and compassion to our fellow inmates, and even the guards—despite how some of them treat us? Those who have a peace about them here in prison, really do stand out.

Let's strive to be witnesses by how we act, and through our actions, show others the love of Jesus.

"Lord, please help me to love the person You put in front of me today. Please let my actions be a witness for You, and my actions to be consistent with what I say."

God Won't Abandon You

> 1 Samuel 12:22: The Lord will not abandon his
> people, because that would dishonor his great
> name. For it has pleased the Lord to make you
> his very own people.

I just received a card delivered to my cell. In the card my aunt wrote, "Please read 1 Samuel 12:22." It's a great verse. I do sometimes feel like I have been rejected by God. Why else would He allow me to be in an accident that has resulted in causing so much pain to others, as well as me doing two-and-a-half-years in jail. I have already spent a year and a half here, and still have a long year to go (apologies to those with more time.) But the Lord has not rejected me. The truth is I am here as a consequence of a decision I made to attempt to drive after drinking. Far from rejecting me, the Lord has blessed me in many ways. He has sent people into my life to help sustain and teach me. I have met people who have given me a whole new perspective on God and His love. No, despite my sin, God has not rejected me. Not only that, He is pleased to make me His own.

There is a man who comes into the jail to conduct Bible studies who is from a family where some of the children are adopted. He talks about how his father was pleased to make these children a part of the family, and made them equals in every respect. He spent the same amount of money on them as his children born to him, sent them all to college, and they are all equal in his will. The children are all fully his, even the adopted ones.

This is true of us with God. Being adopted by God means we have been chosen by Him, and He is pleased to have us as part of his family.

"Lord, thank You for choosing me to be a part of Your family. No matter what I've done, I know You forgive me, and make me an equal heir in your kingdom; I am not rejected by You. I am loved by You and I thank You."

The Promise of Heaven

Revelation 21:27: Nothing impure will ever enter it, nor will anyone who does what is shameful or deceitful, but only those whose names are written in the Lamb's book of life.

The Bible talks about Heaven. I do not know what Heaven will actually look like. I have no idea what we might do there, or what relationships will look like there. These are big questions that have been debated for a long time by people much more educated and wiser than myself. Really I only know two things about Heaven. First, I want to go there. Whatever is in store for us we know we will be with the Lord and it will be glorious. The second thing I know is I am going. The Bible says that if we accept Jesus as our Lord and Savior our names are written in the Book of Life. We can be assured that regardless of our past, no matter what sins we have committed, no matter how much of our lives we spent doing the wrong things or locked up behind bars, once we accept Jesus, our names are written in the Book, and our salvation and place in Heaven is assured. I often daydream of what life will be like when I get out of jail. I imagine it will be wonderful. But really, I know there will be all the same challenges life has always had. It won't be perfect. It won't be perfect until I reach the gates of Heaven.

"Lord, thank You that You have reserved a place for me in Heaven. Please help me live my life really understanding that life here is temporary, and since it is temporary, help me to live for You."

Being Free in Prison

Psalm 116:16: Truly I am your servant, Lord; I serve you just as my mother did; you have freed me from my chains.

The chaplain here the other day was telling us about a lifer at San Quentin. "He is one of the most beautiful and peaceful people I have ever met." He told me that although this person will never get out of San Quentin he is truly free. It's ironic but true. In prison, even though you may be behind bars and occasionally placed in chains, it's also a place many men find freedom. Here you can be free of drugs, and even though you may be reminded of it, you can be free from the shame of your past. You can learn to be free from the fear that haunts us in relationships—fear of closeness and fear of being emotionally hurt like so many of us have been while growing up. They may lock up our bodies; but only we can lock up our minds. So if we choose to let our minds be free, we can learn, we can change, we can find peace and joy, even in prison.

God wants to free us from the chains of our past hurts and guilt and shame. If we let him, no matter what our sentence, we can be truly free.

"God, even though I am locked in a 10 x 6 cell, thank You that I am free in Christ. My mind is free and clear. My spirit is not broken. I am free of the sins of my past, and I am free from guilt and shame which led me to make so many bad decisions in the past. Thank You. I am truly free."

Living Without Fear of Authority

Romans 13:3: For rulers hold no terror for those who do right, but for those who do wrong. Do you want to be free from fear of the one in authority? Then do what is right and you will be commended.

Many of my fellow inmates in County Jail have told me they would rather do more prison time than have a lengthy probation term. They fear, based on past experience, that if they are on probation, they are doomed to come back. Others would rather take more time than take a felony strike, as California has tough mandatory sentencing laws for anyone receiving a 3rd strike. They are afraid of the authorities and what will happen to them if they are busted again and get that third strike.

But you don't need to be afraid of a three-strike law if you never commit another felony. You don't need to be afraid of a p-test if you are living clean. In fact, I have heard many stories of probation and parole being cut short because of good behavior. If we act like good citizen, we do not need to be afraid of those in authority. While I do not like having my cell torn apart and "inspected," I know I don't need to worry about a write-up as I have no contraband. When we do the right thing, we can live confidently and don't have to be afraid.

"Lord, help me to live a clean and productive life. Keep me from temptations that could get me into trouble either in here, or on the outside. Help me to do the right thing, and have no reason to fear authorities."

Not Knowing Why

John 6:66-68: From this time many of his disciples turned back and no longer followed him.
You do not want to leave too, do you?" Jesus
asked the Twelve. Simon Peter answered him,
"Lord, to whom shall we go? You have the
words of eternal life.

There are many things about God I do not understand. I
think every believer I know here in jail has prayed for
mercy from the court. Some have received mercy—a
light or modified sentence, and some who had great faith received harsh sentences.

There are many deep, theological questions, why is there so
much suffering in the world? How does God treat those who
have never heard about him? Do people who sincerely seek
God, but are born in a culture with a different religion, go to
Heaven? Many people with differing opinions on these questions are convinced they are right and quote scripture to prove
they are right, but they cannot all be right.

There are a lot of things about God I'm not sure about. He is
beyond my understanding. In the story of Job, God never tells
Job the reason for his suffering. God tells Job His ways are
beyond Job's comprehension. Not knowing the answer, though,
is not an excuse for turning away from God. Just because we do
not know the answers to some questions does not mean there are
no answers. Our faith does not require God to reveal everything

to us nor does it require us to have all the answers. The one thing we do know for certain is God loves us and wants the best for us. We also know He wants us to love others. Even if I don't know all the answers, if I know for certain God loves me, where else could I go where I could get a better deal than that? Don't turn away from God just because you don't have all the answers.

"God, even though I don't have all the answers to life and there is so much I don't understand, thank You for showing me Your great love. Thank You for loving me even though I have done things that put me in jail. Please help me to trust You even though there is so much about life I do not understand."

Be Still in the Lord, Not Busy

Isaiah 30:15: "In repentance and rest is your salvation, in quietness and trust is your strength, but you would have none of it."

I often think I need to do more. Sometimes I feel obligated to try and make every minute of the day productive. "Make every minute count," the saying goes. But being busy isn't the same as being productive. One of the lessons I have learned while in jail is there are a lot of things I need to let go of.

Often, I need to let go of being worried about results. We get consumed with numbers that we think validate our efforts. For example, we think when a lot of inmates attend our Bible Study that it's "successful" and blessed by God. Maybe, but I think God cares about the quality of the meeting more than how many people are there. It's important to remember God can use us but doesn't need us. If He wants something done, He can get it done. Often He is calling us to stop organizing, striving, and measuring everything we do. Instead, He is calling us to just sit quietly and rest in His peace and love.

There are always many good things that need to get done. But it's in the rest and quietness that I find God, and the strength to carry on.

"Lord, help me not to be so busy that I miss time with You. Help me to rest in You and be quiet and listen. Help me to remember that You want me, not need me to get things done."

God Has a Plan for You

Jeremiah 29:11: "For I know the plans I have
for you," declares the Lord, "plans to prosper
you and not to harm you, plans to give you hope
and a future."

This is the verse and promise from God that I have most
clung to since I've been here. It's also a verse I try to share
with brothers going for sentencing while I am here in County
Jail.

We do not always have to understand the plans God has for us.
It's hard to imagine prison is a part of those plans—I'm sure it
wasn't His initial plan for me, but my decisions and actions
brought me here. But despite this, I know He loves us and
wants to give us a new and brighter future. He wants to prosper
us.

Prospering us does not mean having a lot of money, but He
surely wants to prosper our relationships with Him and others.
If we stay connected to Him, we can do that. The closer I am
to Him, the easier I find it to get along with my sons, ex-wife,
and friends on the outside. I have more patience, and am more
ready to listen. I also get along better with other inmates. He
surely prospers our relationships.

God also gives us hope and a future. Most of us have a release
date, even if it's a long ways away. If we do the right things
while we are here and stay close to God, our future can be very

bright indeed. I know inmates who have obtained college degrees and are now getting out and getting good jobs. If we stay with the Lord, the future is wide open.

"Lord, please help me never to lose hope in the future. I face a lot of obstacles here during my remaining time, and there will also be many obstacles and temptations when I get out. But I know You have plans to make me a better father, friend, and person. Please help me to live that future and do everything I can now to prepare for it."

Become a Listener

James 1:19: My dear brothers and sisters, take note of this: Everyone should be quick to listen, slow to speak and slow to become angry,

It's December here in the jail and we just had a Catholic speaker come in and give us an interesting challenge for the next year. He asked us to pick a word, or phrase, and use that when we are stressed, angry, or need a reminder to act in a kind way. For example, we might use "relax," or "no fear," to remind us when we are afraid to do the right thing, to do it anyway.

As he spoke, I knew right away I wanted my word for next year to be "listen." I want to constantly remind myself to listen—to listen to God; listen to the world around me; listen to myself when I feel emotions arising within me, and especially listen to others. How often, when "engaged" in a conversation with someone, do I realize I am simply thinking about what I want to say as soon as the other person pauses? And I hate to admit it, but in group settings, I often find myself judging what others are saying instead of really listening to what they have to say and trying to understand where they are coming from. Instead, I want to *start showing love by giving people my full attention.*

Being mindful and present in the moment is usually simply about listening—really listening, to the world around me. And, of course, to hear God, we often need to be still and meditate on His Word, really listening.

"Lord, please give me ears so I can listen, really listen, to You and to those around me. Please help me not to be distracted by my ego and so concerned with what I want to say so that I don't hear the person in front of me. Instead, please help me to generously give my full attention to anyone speaking to me. And when my thoughts start to wander, please gently bring to my mind, the word "listen."

Making Prison Good for You

Isaiah 39:17: Yes, this anguish was good for me, for you have rescued me from death and forgiven all my sins.

I've been in jail now for almost two years. In this time, I've learned a lot—a lot about myself, about other people, and God. I'm also clean and sober. While the tragedy that brought me here affected many people, and I lost my job, life savings, and the respect of many people, I've also gained. I've gained a new perspective and a new chance at life. I've lost precious time with my sons that I will never get back, but at the same time, I now realize how precious every moment with them is. I've lost my life savings, but I've learned I cannot rely on money, and to be satisfied with much less. I've lost the legal right to drink alcohol, but I've gained the freedom to not drink.

Because of the other people involved, I can never say this experience was worth it. But I do hope to look back one day and be grateful for all the lessons I learned during my time in jail. In fact, I am already thankful for all that God has taught me through this. I pray that one day my family looks back and is grateful not for what happened, but for the changed man I became.

"Lord, as hard as it's been, this experience has benefited me. Let these changes in me take root and become permanent. Please let me never forget what You have taught me while I've been incarcerated, and now, help me to live in such a way I benefit others and never go back to being who I once was."

Staying Calm

Proverbs 12:16: Fools show their annoyance at once, but the prudent overlook an insult.

I spent a few weeks in a twelve-man tank. At one point, a group of men of another race wanted to change places with the men of my race and told us we had to switch bunks. Some of the men of my race wanted to refuse, or at least get the key holder involved. They were afraid if we got punked on this issue, it would lead to us to being vulnerable to potential abuse, and the other group might threaten us in other ways.

Prison politics is different everywhere and it may have different "rules and realities" where you are. But in this case, I argued it wasn't worth a potential write-up or fight. It certainly wasn't something worth doing more time for. I argued we should make the changes based on their seniority and let the issue go, which we ultimately did. Plus, we are in County so we are likely to change cells soon anyway.

I know a guy who recently got into a prison fight and hit a guy, and as the guy went down, he hit his head on a table and almost died. So the guy I know is facing a significant new charge on top of a fifteen-year sentence. Another friend, awaiting to see his counselor in reception, just got a 115 (California write-up for fighting) and may have lost his chance to go to fire camp. In both cases, the person felt disrespected because of what someone said. We all know the importance of respect where we are at. But we always need to keep in mind what our goal is—for most of us, it's to get home to our families as soon as possible. We need to show respect for them by keeping out of the mix.

"Lord, help me to show respect and love to my fellow inmates. And, when I feel disrespected, really help me to think before I act. Often, like me, the other man is hiding behind fear or pain. Help me to realize that and be able to help others. Above all, please help me control my temper."

Grateful for Safety

Psalm 31:21: Praise be to the Lord, for he showed me the wonders of his love when I was in a city under siege.

P rison is certainly a city under siege. We constantly have to maneuver through racial politics, adhere to strict codes of "respect," and avoid those guards that are abusive. But even here, living under siege, God shows us the wonders of His love. There are many mercies granted to us by Him, even if the judicial system doesn't grant us any. I think about some of the people I've met here, chaplains, inspiring speakers, and inmates, all who have helped me grow and become a better person.

I keep a gratitude journal and each day record things I am grateful for and why. As I look back over my journal, I see God has provided for me and cared for me, even while I'm locked up. This journey has not been easy. It has not been painless, but as I look back I can see God has been with me—helping me, prodding me, teaching me, blessing me—showing me the wonders of His love.

"Lord, thank You for not abandoning me while I'm here. Thank you for the opportunities where I'm at to attend classes, and learn about myself and You. Thank You for keeping me safe, and thank You for helping me make it through another day."

Jesus Is Our Water

Jeremiah 2:13: "My people have committed two sins: They have forsaken me, the spring of living water, and have dug their own cisterns, broken cisterns that cannot hold water.

Jesus is the living water we need. In Him we can find fulfillment and it is only through Him that we can find our true selves, the person who we were created to be. The person we can be if we do not act out of shame, guilt, or fear. But instead of coming to Him to quench our thirst, we build our own wells. We build wells of money, power, or drugs to try and make us happy. But, in the end, we become a slave to these things, and for many of us, these wells result in us coming to prison. In prison we might seek safety in gangs, money through a hustle, or relief through drugs or pruno. In the end though, these often lead to an endless cycle of more trouble and more pain. If we want to truly be happy and free, we must abandon the false wells we create and seek the living water of Jesus. In Him we can break free of addictions and destructive habits. We can have a life that's truly free. We can be free to be our true selves as He created us to be, even if we are confined to prison walls.

"Lord, please help me to see that the wells I create will never quench my thirst. Please give me Your living water and help me to be the person You created me to be."

Start Living Now

Zachariah 4:10: "Who dares despise the day of
small things, since the seven eyes of the Lord
that range throughout the earth will rejoice
when they see the chosen capstone in the hand
of Zerubbabel?"

Most days in jail or prison are pretty routine. So much
so that, when inmates get out, they often have a
hard time adjusting to the pace and variety of life
on the outside. Here in County, I know what I'll be doing pretty
much every hour of the day. Sure, during rec I'll have to make
a decision about either working out, watching a movie, or playing chess. But even then, I have my routines and habits, so it's
pretty much a given on what I will choose to do.

But each day doesn't need to be just one more day to get
through until we get out so we can "start to live." We need to
start to live now. It's true that today nothing exciting or different may happen, but God says not to "despise the day of small
things." Our lives are built brick-by-brick, and God rejoices
when he sees us add another brick of positivity in our lives.
Today, maybe we go to a twelve-step meeting and add a brick
to recovery, or read our Bible and pray and add a brick to our
relationship with God, or sign up for a class to add a brick to
our education. Maybe we spend some time with someone who
needs some encouragement and help that person add a brick to
their foundation.

If we keep doing the right thing, brick-by-brick, one small action by one small action, we can change our lives, and God sees and blesses each of these bricks.

"Lord, today is the 704th day I've been in jail, and it seems like every other day—a small day. But please help me to add another brick to my foundation in my new life with You, and please bless that brick."

Attitude of Gratitude

Psalm 23:5: You prepare a table before me in the presence of my enemies. You anoint my head with oil; my cup overflows.

P rison can be a violent and lonely place. We all know that. Even the strongest among us are constantly tested—physically, mentally, and spiritually. But it's also possible to feel peace and joy in prison. There are times, although they may be rare, that I feel strangely content and at peace. There are times I can let my guard down and be open and vulnerable to a few select people. There are times I am able to rise above all the politics and codes of respect and see people for how they really are. In those times I see a bunch of men who, like me, are hurting and afraid; and in those times, I am less hurting and afraid. I'm often asked how I keep from getting annoyed by others here or depressed at my situation. I tell people it's usually because I choose to have an attitude of gratitude. Victor Frankel, the survivor of a Nazi Concentration Camp once wrote "The last freedom we have is to change our attitude."

To me, this doesn't mean pretending to be happy when we are not. It means, despite our circumstances, we look for and appreciate the small blessings we receive each day. When we do that two things happen. First, others take notice, and we develop a positive reputation. Secondly, we are better able to face it through each day, even when that day is in jail or prison.

"Lord, thank you for the blessings you have provided me here while I am in jail. Thank you that through Jesus you provide me an island of peace in this ocean of suffering and despair."

Joy Amidst a Terrible Sentence

Malachi 4:2: But for you who revere my name, the sun of righteousness will rise with healing in its rays. And you will go out and frolic like well-fed calves.

A friend of mine that I've been here in County with for over two years will soon be sentenced for a second-degree murder charge which carries fifteen to life. Today at Bible Study, this brother shared that last month, when he was in a holding tank during jury deliberation, he was praying, and for the first time in his life things started to make sense to him. He felt God's presence, and God was saying to him that no matter what the verdict, it was going to be all right. When the jury came back and delivered a guilty verdict, it didn't faze him. He was disappointed to be sure, but he also felt his life now had a clearer purpose and focus. He knew now that even while locked up, he would now focus on helping others, and try to prevent more tragedies like the drunk driving accident that brought him here. While here in jail, he has become a Peacemaker's Alliance Facilitator and learned he has leadership skills and teaching qualities. Skills and qualities he intends to use in prison.

Although he is facing a life sentence, my friend is free. And when you talk to him, you can tell he has been healed of his fears, addictions, and the broken relationships of his past. The healing gives him freedom, peace, and even joy, despite his impending sentence. When he talks about what God has done for him, I see courage, hope, and peace. Like the verse above says, I see a well-fed calf frolicking in the pasture.

"Lord, please help my brother as he faces his sentence and future. Please let the court see his heart and be merciful. Let those of us who know You, even those of us behind bars, experience the joy that comes from You, and let us frolic like well-fed calves."

Who Are You Looking For?

John 20:13-15: They asked her, "Woman, why are you crying?" "They have taken my Lord away," she said, "and I don't know where they have put him." At this, she turned around and saw Jesus standing there, but she did not realize that it was Jesus. He asked her, "Woman, why are you crying? Who is it you are looking for?" Thinking he was the gardener, she said, "Sir, if you have carried him away, tell me where you have put him, and I will get him."

We have plans. We think things are going to go a certain way, but they don't. Things go wrong—horribly wrong. We get arrested. We become upset. We become angry. But Jesus sees us and asks, "Who/what are you looking for?" Maybe we were looking for money. Maybe we were looking to get high to escape from the pain and reality of our lives. Maybe we were looking to belong to something and joined a gang or group of friends that led us into trouble.

Even here in jail we may still be searching. We might join a gang, or seek out drugs. We might look for any way we can to escape the tedium and routine of a jail cell. But no matter what we do, no matter what we turn to, Jesus is right here, asking us who we are looking for. And if we could just see clearly, we would recognize Him. He is right in front of us trying to help us, but we don't see Him or maybe we choose not to see Him because we think He has abandoned us or because things didn't go our way. But the reality is, He's had a better plan all along. The disciples didn't understand Jesus had to die and would be resurrected. Is it possible we don't understand we had to go to jail or prison so God could get our attention and teach us something?

"Lord, I've spend a lot of my life searching for something and not even knowing what I was looking for. Thank you that you've been here all along. I know now that I was looking for you."

Renewing Your Spirit

2 Corinthians 4:16: Therefore we do not lose
heart. Though outwardly we are wasting
away, yet inwardly we are being renewed
day by day.

I received a letter yesterday from a friend who started the
letter by apologizing for not coming to visit. She con-
fessed she was scared to come and see me "in this condition." I wrote back that she didn't need to worry so much
about me. While it's true parts of my life are on hold, I told
her I am in a better emotional and spiritual place than I had
been in years. Yes, we waste away in a jail/prison, and are getting older, but this can also be a time of great growth if we
choose to work on ourselves. While it is often noisy, I have
time early in the morning to meditate, read the Bible, and pray.
This habit sets the tone for my day. I also use my time to read
a lot of spiritual books I know I wouldn't have read on the outside. I've expanded my views by talking to men of other faiths
and backgrounds, something else I never did on the outside.

Yes, I am getting older here and missing some years I wish I
didn't have to spend behind bars, but my mind and spiritual
walk are getting stronger. And each day the Lord renews my
strength and helps me to face my day so I don't lose heart.

*"Lord, help me not to view my time in jail as wasted years. For
I know if I become closer to you the time is not wasted at all.*

Please help me to take advantage of the time to improve my mind and my relationship with you."

Remembering the Lessons

> Deuteronomy 6:12: be careful that you do not forget the Lord, who brought you out of Egypt, out of the land of slavery.

I am now "short to the house." I've completed ninety percent of my time, and in a few months I will finally be free and allowed to leave. I hope and pray I will keep the many lessons I have learned close to me and not forget them. But as the saying goes, "There are two trash cans outside of every jail, one for canes and one for Bibles." Why is it so many of us leave only to come right back? Right now, waiting to come up to my programming POD is a former inmate who had been here for over a year, and has only been out a couple months and is now facing a new and serious charge.

For me, there are a couple keys that I hope will keep me from coming back. One, is to surround myself with others who are supportive—through church and a recovery community. Never underestimate how powerful an influence those around us are on our behavior. Sticking close and making friends with people doing the right thing is essential.

I've also engraved a few key images in my mind to remind me of this painful experience. One image in particular stands out to me. My son was visiting me, and as I was talking with him, with glass between us, a tear rolled down his cheek. To see him so sad and knowing both that I caused his pain and I could not reach out and hug him to comfort him, broke my heart. Even though it was a painful image, I committed it to my memory. Whenever I am tempted to do something wrong, I bring this image back to my mind and remember how badly he and I felt. I can never let anything happen to put us in that situation again.

"Lord, help me not to ever forget the lessons You taught me here while I was in jail, and how You stood with me and protected me. Surround me with others who believe in You and help me so I never lose my freedom again."

Impress with Love, Not Knowledge

1 Corinthians 8:1b-2: We know that "We all possess knowledge." But knowledge puffs up while love builds up. Those who think they know something do not yet know as they ought to know.

I really appreciate the Bible studies we have here in County Jail, but one thing I've noticed is a lot of inmates, particularly when they are new, seem to try to impress others with their knowledge of the Bible or spiritual facts. It's great that they join right in, but it also seems some come in wanting to be known as a "jailhouse preacher" and impress the rest of us with their knowledge. And to be fair, a lot of them do have an impressive amount of Bible knowledge.

But God is not impressed with what we know, even if it is Bible facts. Compared to the Maker of the Universe, we know very little—in fact, next to nothing. Even if we do know a lot and can impress our fellow inmates, so what? A lot of times we say things not to help others, but so we can look smart. But, as opposed to knowledge, love is different. Love does not puff us up; it edifies others. Also, when we show love to others, not only does it bring us closer to them, it brings us closer to God. Knowledge, may, even if we don't mean it to, separate us from others, but love brings us together. Yes, we need to learn, but the most important thing we need to learn is how to love others.

"Lord, help me not to use what I know to try to impress others and build myself up. Instead, please help me to use kindness to demonstrate the love you've shown me."

I Am Praying for You

1 Samuel 12:23: As for me, far be it that I should sin against the Lord by failing to pray for you. And I will teach you the way that is good and right.

Doing time in jail or prison is hard. I know, I've done it. Some places require you to be constantly alert; letting your awareness down could result in serious consequences. Even if you are not on a dangerous yard, and even if there are no threats of violence, it's still a very lonely place. Time passes slowly, and it's almost impossible not to be filled with regrets of the past. Relationships with people on the outside are hard to maintain, and you often find yourself at the mercy of others. Guards have a tremendous amount of control over you, and unless family or friends supply our needs by putting money on our books, we go without.

But we can get through this time. If we work on our relationship with God, our time is not wasted. We can be a light to others to show them there is hope, rest, and peace in Jesus. And you are not alone—you are not alone! There are people praying for you. I know this is true because I am praying for you, and I will continue to pray for you every day until you are out or I can no longer pray. God bless you!

"Lord, please be with my brothers and sisters who are still in jail. No matter what brought us here, help us to know You love us and care for us. Please protect everyone reading these words,

give them the strength and hope to make it through the day. Bless them, dear Lord, and show them You are real. Amen."

Washing Feet

John 13:5 and 13:14: After that, he poured water
into a basin and began to wash his disciples' feet,
drying them with the towel that was wrapped
around him. Now that I, your Lord and Teacher,
have washed your feet, you also should wash one
another's feet.

This morning during my meditation time, an image of Jesus
washing his disciples' feet came to me. I began to image what that
would be like. I then imaged Jesus in my cell washing my feet.
This was both awkward and humbling.

Later, I was in a meeting and someone was talking, and I
found myself judging his comments, and as he kept going, I
was thinking to myself, *I wish he would stop.* But then the
image came back to me and I wondered, "What would it mean
to wash this person's feet?" Right now it means listening to
him, really listening, and trying to understand where he is
coming from.

Still later, another inmate asked me to help him with some of
his homework and I hesitated, as to be honest, I didn't want
to use my rec time to help him; I felt like going to play chess
instead—but then I realized this was an opportunity to wash
his feet. Jesus tells us to simply do as he did. Be fully present
and be willing to help others and be humble. If he can wash my
feet, can't I find ways to wash the feet of my fellow inmates?

"Lord, thank You that You were willing to humble yourself and come to earth to wash my feet by dying for me. Please show me the opportunities to wash the feet of everyone I meet, especially those here in jail with me."

Miscellaneous Writings

A collection of random writings I wrote during my time in County Jail.

To My Friends and Family

September 22, 2017

TO MY FRIENDS AND FAMILY, FROM RANDY:
AN UPDATE ON SENTENCING

As you have probably heard by now, on the 20th, after 17 months here in County Jail, I was sentenced to an additional year in County Jail and five years' probation.

Despite local media reports, I am not eligible to be released before that. I will be here for another full twelve months. I thank God I was spared having to go to State Prison, or do more time than that.

I wanted you all to know how eternally grateful I am for your support, letters, encouragement, and prayers during this process. I went to church all my life, and studied religion in college but never truly understood the love of Jesus until it was demonstrated by those of you who rallied around me, despite knowing the worst about me. Some of you may not consider yourselves representatives of Jesus, but you all have the values of love and compassion. I have felt that when I needed it the most, and it came from you. Thank you. I look forward to reconnecting with you one day.

For now, please let my experience remind you what a gift every day is. Hug someone, forgive someone, and apologize to someone. Laugh at things that irritate you—bad weather, traffic, broken shoelaces. Know that none of that matters— none of that remains. Love remains; family remains; true friends remain.

I love you all,

Randy

The Pain in My Toe

I t's probably a bone spur or calcium deposit. Whatever it is, when I touch the second toe on my right foot in just the right spot, it sends a shooting pain throughout my body. But it's a small spot; so it rarely gets touched, maybe 2-4 times per day. And although it's painful, it's really just an annoyance. Usually, I would just ignore it. I've had these before, and they eventually go away. But the thought occurs to me to pray for my toe. If faith can move mountains, then if I have faith and send positive energy and focus to my toe, I can access the divine power of God to heal my toe, right? But I think this is frivolous. I don't believe in the "prosperity gospel." I don't believe God has nothing better to do than find me a good parking space or heal my annoying toe. So I compromise. I decide when the spot gets touched, as it inevitably will a couple times a day, I will thank God for my otherwise good health and the good health of my two sons. So that's what I do.

And for the next few days whenever I feel the pain, I am reminded of our good health and instead of being mad at my toe, I am thankful to God. But the toe does still hurt. About a week later the pain hasn't subsided, and I give up and decide to focus my energy on my toe. And with all the faith I can muster, I pray, "God, please don't take offense at my selfish request, but please heal my toe." Then I go to bed.

The next morning, I realize I am touching "the spot," but don't feel any pain. I start feeling around trying to locate it. Nothing. I should be amazed and shout for joy, but instead I begin to panic.

I am afraid. I realize I am afraid because the thought of an actual miracle is scary. Did God really heal my toe? I keep feeling around and assume eventually I will find it, and when I feel the pain I will be perhaps disappointed but mostly relieved.

I will be relieved to know God does not literally interact with me. I will be able to continue in the knowledge that although I believe God can do miracles, miracles happen to other people in far-away places. I do not have to face the incredible implication that God might do miracles in my life, and therefore, He does truly exist, and He is very near. A God who could and would interact with me for even simple requests implies a whole new way of looking at Him, a whole different kind of faith.

The implication is staggering—not for my toe, but for my life. I've always believed in God, but have somewhat kept him at arm's length. My faith has always been sincere, yet not enough to move me to take action to do all the good things I consider doing. He's always been real to me, but on an intellectual, reserved, church-on-Sunday kind of way.

Now, as I am feeling around trying to find the painful spot on my toe, I understand why people who encountered the power of Jesus ask Him to leave (Mark 5:17). Really, truly coming face-to-face with Jesus' power means one will have to change, and that's scary.

As I continue searching for that painful spot on my toe, I am realizing how I need to change. I need to believe in a personal Jesus and powerful God who loves me, and cares about me, and interacts with me. If I truly, really believe that, I know my whole life will change.

So did I ever find the pain spot or did God miraculously make my toe better? It doesn't matter because God truly healed me in more important ways that morning.

Reflective Essay

Note: This is a reflective essay I wrote for a communications class while in jail.

> Philippians 1:19: For I know that through your prayers and God's provision of the Spirit of Jesus Christ what has happened to me will turn out for my deliverance"

Unleashing creativity by creating a "mistake-driven culture" is a popular business mantra these days. In fact, it's one I've adopted myself. My adoption is ironic, however, given the immense shame I feel when I fail at something, or sense others may believe I've failed. Failure is so shameful to me, I will attempt to justify, explain away, excuse, or even deny to the point of dishonesty if an accomplishment of mine is deemed or judged as subpar. It is, therefore, unconscionable to me and cause for much personal pain to have failed in such a dramatic, complete, and public way, and as a result, to be enduring the further shame of incarceration. Unlike past failures, this one cannot be justified, excused, or covered up for this tragic failure has severe consequences affecting many people and has been broadcast to a wide and public audience.

This event, then, obliterates the image of success I had crafted for others to believe, and came to believe myself. No longer will I be admired as the "golden boy" of the family, or the successful, seasoned, conservative, Christian executive who so rarely makes a mistake or failed at anything. Rather now, a simple Google search attaches new labels to my name: "alco-holic, drunk driver, irresponsible," even "murderer."

With the two images of myself juxtaposed—the one I tried to create and the new one publicly available—a third more honest one emerges. While in some ways I was someone many people considered to be successful, I was also in many ways morally and spiritually lacking. I attended church regularly, but I lacked an active, deeply-committed faith. I used alcohol to re-lieve stress and pressure, including or especially, the pressure to not fail rather than face life's challenges head on. I allowed my relationship with my wife to completely deteriorate, and although my boys and I have always been close, I robbed them by drinking and not always being fully present.

Having now more honestly interpreted my past, I can begin to shape a new self-perspective for the future. Freed of the burden of being perfect, and unlikely to ever fail so dramatically as I have now, I see a middle way. I am now free to explore spirit-uality without the burden of being "morally upright," as no confession I can make will shock anyone more than my now public sins. Likewise, I am now free to join a recovery com-munity without having to hide that part of my life—it is now assumed by all that I need to be a part of that group. I am now also free to engage in deeper, more meaningful relationships with more honest dialogue, for the friends that I still have, have been tested. I know they are true and loyal. They know the worst about me, and yet have stood by me. Thus, I know I am free to be completely myself with them.

It's impossible to know how the narrative of the second half of my life will unfold. But I do foresee a more honest, bolder, more authentic version of myself emerging. I see for the first time that my mistakes and failings are not my shame, but rather my healing and redemption.

To My Son Nicholas On His Birthday

Not because you are smart and can ace any test
But because you think about important issues.

Not because you win elections,
But because you dare to run.

Not because you're willing to look and be different,
But because you're willing to be yourself.

Not because of what you accomplish,
But because of who you are.

Because you kept going when I gave you a reason to quit,
Because you inspire me and help me be a better me.

You are who you are meant to be,
And I love you.

Nick, you have what it takes, you're good enough, you're strong enough, and you're man enough.

Happy 20th Birthday son.
I love you.
Dad

To My Son Christopher On His Birthday

Not because you're the lead,
But because you dare to get on stage.

Not because you can fool people with magic,
But because you practice and practice to perfect your craft.

Not because you scored touchdowns and hit homeruns,
But because when you dropped, passed, and struck out—you didn't quit.

Because you kept going when I made it hard on you,
Because you encourage me and help me to be a better me.

Because you are who you were meant to be,

I love you.

Chris, you have what it takes, you're good enough, you're strong enough, and you're man enough.

Happy 16th Birthday Son.
I love you.
Dad

To My Mother on Mother's Day

May 2017

Mom,

How does one express how they feel about one's mother? How does one thank a mother?

Mom, you have raised me, taught me, encouraged me, and loved me. We count on a mother to love and support us when no one else does, to believe in us when no one else will. But rarely are mothers actually put through that test. But mom, you have been. In the unpredictable experiences of life, I suddenly found myself on the wrong side of judgement. At that time, I was painfully aware of my mistakes, well aware of my failures, and had plenty of people reminding me of them. But you didn't. You stood by me, helped me, supported me, and encouraged me, while others abandoned me. When I needed you most you, loved me.

I have known and been confident of your love for me all my life. But until recently, I never really understood what that meant, or how much I needed it. But now I do.

Thank you. I love you.
Randy

Closing Thoughts

All these writings were done during the two and a half years I spent in County Jail. That was an incredibly painful time for me, but also a time of tremendous growth and spiritual renewal. I wrote these by hand and sent them to my mother who would type them up and send them back to me. It was a way for us to stay in touch and for her to know what I was thinking about from a spiritual perspective. At the time, I did not think I would publish them. But I have been encouraged to tell parts of my story and this is one simple way of doing that. In addition, I owe. I have responsibilities to those I've hurt as well as to those who are in jail or prison. This little book doesn't begin to settle my debts, but if it helps anyone, the effort will have been worth it.

Out of respect, I do not mention those who have been hurt by my actions, or give much detail about what brought me to jail. But if you have been hurt by my actions and you are reading this, please know how eternally sorry I am and know that I am praying for you daily. For those of you behind bars, I hope you found some encouragement through these words. I wish I could do more. Please use whatever resources are available to you to help you on your journey. May God bless you during your remaining time. I look forward to meeting you one day on the outside.

— Randy
March 2020

Made in the USA
Las Vegas, NV
23 November 2024